AN END TO POVERTY?

GARETH STEDMAN JONES

AN END TO POVERTY?

A HISTORICAL DEBATE

COLUMBIA UNIVERSITY PRESS   NEW YORK

Columbia University Press
Publishers Since 1893
New York   Chichester, West Sussex

Copyright © Gareth Stedman Jones, 2004
First published by Profile Books Ltd, London

Library of Congress Cataloging-in-Publication Data
A complete CIP record is available from the Library of Congress.
ISBN 0–231–13172–0 (cloth : alk. paper)

♾

Columbia University Press books are printed on permanent and
durable acid-free paper.
Printed in the United States of America

c 10 9 8 7 6 5 4 3 2 1

To my mother

CONTENTS

ACKNOWLEDGEMENTS

This book has been written to accompany the Anglo-American Conference of the Institute of Historical Research, whose theme in 2004 was 'Wealth and Poverty'. I wish to thank the Director of the Institute, David Bates, for encouraging me to undertake this assignment. I would also like to thank Peter Carson, Penny Daniel, Maggie Hanbury, Sally Holloway and Tim Penton for the part they have played in the publication of this book.

The thinking which shaped it is to a large extent the result of discussions and seminars which have taken place at the Centre for History and Economics at King's College, Cambridge since 1992. I wish to thank the John D. and Catherine T. MacArthur Foundation which has so generously supported the activities of the Centre. I have learnt from many who have participated in the intellectual life of the Centre, but especially from Emma Rothschild who provided constant inspiration and encouragement, while I was writing this book. Those who have helped to manage the Centre have also been of invaluable assistance, in particular

Inga Huld Markan, Jo Maybin, Rachel Coffey and Justine Crump.

There are many others who have provided important suggestions, insights or help as this book was being prepared. I would particularly like to mention Robert Tombs, Daniel Pick, Tristram Hunt, Michael Sonenscher, Istvan Hont, David Feldman, Barry Supple, Sally Alexander and Daniel Stedman Jones. Finally, a special thanks to Miri Rubin who persuaded me that it was possible to write this book and did so much to help it towards its completion.

INTRODUCTION

This book employs history to illuminate questions of policy and politics which still have resonance now. It aims to make visible some of the threads by which the past is connected with the present. It does so by bringing to light the first debates, which occurred in the late eighteenth century, about the possibility of a world without poverty. These arguments were no longer about Utopia in an age-old sense. They were inspired by a new question: whether scientific and economic progress could abolish poverty, as traditionally understood. Some of the difficulties encountered were eerily familiar. Many of the problems which politicians and journalists imagine to have arisen in the world only recently – globalisation, financial regulation, downsizing and commercial volatility – were already in the eighteenth century objects of recurrent concern.

It is of course true that the world in which discussion of these issues first arose was very different from our own. It was dominated by the revolutions of 1776 in America and 1789 in France, as well as by the first movements to overcome slavery and empire. The arguments discussed in this book took place in a period which witnessed the overturning of ancient forms of sovereignty across Europe, direct assaults upon monarchy, aristocracy and church, crises of religious belief, the emergence of 'the common people' as an independent political force, and a war fought across all the oceans of the world.

But to a greater degree than we are prone to imagine, those upheavals and their legacy are still relevant to us. Our conceptions of the economy, both national and international, and its relationship to political processes are still in some ways shaped by the conflicts discussed in this book. So are the relationships between religion, citizenship and economic life. Those who doubt the relevance of history because they believe that the world was made anew by the defeat of Communism, the end of the Cold War, and the demise of socialism at the beginning of the 1990s, do not escape its hold. They simply become the guileless consumers of its most simple-minded reconstructions. Those who devised the new reform programmes of post-socialist parties, desperate to remove any residue of an old-fashioned and discredited collectivism, hastened to embrace a deregulated economy hopefully moralised by periodic homilies about communitarian sentiment. By doing this, they imagined themselves to be buying into an unimpeachable and up-to-date liberal tradition handed down in a distinguished lineage of economists and philosophers inspired by the *laisser faire* libertarianism of Adam Smith's *The Wealth of Nations*.

This book reveals that such assumptions are at best dubious and, for the most part, false. The free market individualism of American conservatives and the moral authoritarianism which often accompanies it are not the products of Smith (although they certainly draw selectively upon certain of his formulations), but of the recasting of political economy in the light of the frightened reaction to the republican radicalism of the French Revolution.

Smith's analyses of 'moral sentiments' and commercial society were not the exclusive possession of any one political tendency. The battle to appropriate his mantle was closely intertwined with the battle over the French Revolution itself. Modern commentators are agreed that Smith was not in any distinctive or meaningful sense a Christian, while those who wrote about him at the time strongly suspected it; worse still, at least for contemporaries, the evidence provided by his revisions to the 1790 edition of *The Theory of Moral Sentiments*, which he had originally written in 1759, suggested that at the end of his life he was even less of a Christian than before. This was not merely a minor or incidental quirk in Smith's picture of the world, it informed his fundamental conception of human motivation as well as his theory of history. In *The Theory of Moral Sentiments*, Smith wrote of the ambition which drove on 'the poor man's son' to strive to become rich and, if successful, to advertise his newfound status by procuring 'mere trinkets of frivolous utility'. After a disquisition on the impossibility of translating wealth into happiness, Smith concluded:

> Power and riches appear then to be, what they are,
> enormous and operous machines contrived to produce a
> few trifling conveniences to the body, consisting of springs
> the most nice and delicate, which must be kept in order
> with the most anxious attention, and which in spite of all
> our care are ready every moment to burst into pieces, and
> crush in their ruins their unfortunate possessor.

Nevertheless, he continued, 'It is well that nature imposes
on us in this manner. It is this deception which rouses and
keeps in continual motion the industry of mankind.'[1]

The idea that some kind of trick or self-deception was the
basic motivating factor behind human activity, but that it
was nevertheless to be cherished – because it explained why
mankind was induced to 'found cities and commonwealths,
and to invent and improve all the sciences and arts, which
ennoble and embellish human life' – was difficult to inte-
grate either into Christianity or into what in the years after
1789 was presented as a post-Christian republican alternative. Smith's picture derived from classical sources, part stoic
and part epicurean. It sat ill with Christian evangelicalism.
Nor did it accord well with counter- or post-revolutionary
apologias for aristocracies, merchants, established churches,
low wages or the outlawing of combinations of labourers.
But then nor could it be said to endorse republicanism,
egalitarianism, democratic representation or the toppling
of aristocracies. Supporters and opponents of the Revolution, therefore, annexed different parts of Smith's picture

of commercial society to support rival visions of social and political life.

This story of the bifurcation of Smith's legacy is relevant to the present. On the one side, anti-republicans married a version of Smith to a bleak possessive individualism underpinned by Christian evangelical theology. This authoritarian but anti-paternalist philosophy was elaborated into what became known in Britain as 'liberal Toryism' and it remained dominant in the 'Treasury view' of economic and welfare policy from the aftermath of the battle of Waterloo down to the criticisms of Keynes and the end of the gold standard in 1931.[2] In modified form, parts of it have survived and continue today in the neo-conservative ethos of American Republicanism.

One extreme bred another. It was this conservative and anti-utopian transformation of political economy which in turn produced by way of reaction the genesis of revolutionary socialism. Especially influential was Malthus's *Essay on the Principle of Population* of 1798. The population theory provided the main bulwark against further attempts to enlarge the framework of collective welfare provision for around a century. Furthermore, its replacement, both in economic theory and in social policy of a language of civil society and political participation by a language of 'natural forces', legitimated and institutionalised a fear and suspicion of the 'labouring poor' which the reaction against the Revolution had already done so much to intensify.

For conservatives, the Revolution was almost from the

5

beginning a demonstration of the fallacy of ignoring the primacy of the passions over reason in human affairs. In the course of the 1790s, this outlook, deeply rooted in Christian assumptions about original sin, was translated into the terms made available by the Newtonian language of natural theology and was extended into the sphere of sexual gratification. By treating reproduction as a biological imperative and the primal driving force behind the activities of the mass of humanity, past, present and future, Malthus subordinated all history, law and culture to an instinctual non-social and ahistorical force. Once this conception had been implanted at the heart of political economy, the core of economics was henceforth situated in the realm of nature. It was for this reason that a crude behavioural approach to human psychology came to be considered the appropriate method in the development of economic theory.

What this ignored was the fact that observed regularities in the process of production, consumption and exchange, far from belonging to nature, were only possible when such transactions were regulated according to law and custom. It was for this reason that Hegel, who was a careful reader of Smith, treated the emergence of 'civil society' and the formalisation of its anatomy in political economy as distinctive products of the modern world. For 'civil society' presupposed a set of legal and cultural norms within which a 'system of needs' could develop. It presupposed the overthrow of the violence and arbitrariness of slavery and feudalism.

In Germany, Hegel's optimistic and moderately progressive picture of civil society was also pushed on to the defensive by a combination of fundamentalist pietism, aristocratic reaction, possessive individualism and a romantic reassertion of the divine right of monarchy.[3] Marx's redescription of Hegel's conception of civil society, what he called 'the capitalist mode of production', also therefore drew more upon Malthus than upon Smith and Hegel in its depiction of the economy. The economy was depicted as an arena in which man had become dominated by his own creations and had reverted to a language of 'natural forces' to describe his relations with his fellow beings. As Marx wrote to Engels about *The Origin of the Species* in 1862:

> It is remarkable how Darwin rediscovers, among the beasts and plants, the society of England with its division of labour, competition, opening up of new markets, 'inventions' and Malthusian 'struggle for existence'. It is Hobbes' *bellum omnium contra omnes* [the struggle of all against all] and is reminiscent of Hegel's *Phenomenology* in which civil society figures as an 'intellectual animal kingdom', whereas, in Darwin, the animal kingdom figures as civil society.[4]

Thus, both in the dominant language of political economy and, perversely, in what was to become the most influential critique of political economy, a strange consensus conspired to push the legal, institutional and cultural dimensions of the analysis of commercial society to the margins.

∽

Could there have been an alternative to this conservative trajectory and the revolutionary communism it provoked in response? What of the use that the republican support- ers of enlightenment and the Revolution, Antoine-Nicolas Condorcet and Thomas Paine, made of Smith and other advances in the eighteenth-century moral and social sciences, to form the social underpinnings of a viable republic? As this book makes clear in its discussion of the reaction to the proposals of Condorcet and Paine in anti-Jacobin England and post-Jacobin France, such an alternative was virtually smothered at birth. Even when its protagonists were not literally burnt in effigy – as Paine was all over England in the early 1790s – or pushed like Condorcet to a premature death, their proposals were radically misrepresented. Nor was there a strong constituency pushing for such policies among those supporting the ideals of the Revolution. Mod- erates simply hoped that post-1789 France would resemble post-1688 England. But among those still pressing for reform at home, Smith was henceforward harnessed together with Malthus. Those who seriously questioned this equation were relegated to a romantic twilight zone beyond the pale of respectable economics. Conversely, for those on the left of the Revolution, the proposals associated with Paine and Condorcet were considered too respectful of commerce and private property to be of use. Nor did the situation greatly improve in the two centuries following 1789. The tax and welfare policies of Condorcet and Paine, when not wholly forgotten, were only recalled as oddities of no programmatic relevance. Later proposals for national insurance and old age pensions drew upon other sources of inspiration and were designed to attain different political aims.

In the twentieth century, the tradition which pushed the interpretation of Smith rightwards, from Hayek to Himmelfarb, built up a strong and elaborate case resting, among other things, upon an old-fashioned respect for historical scholarship.[5] By contrast, the left, which was reluctantly forced to retreat from Marxism, often seems drawn towards the abandonment of any detailed engagement with the historical terrain at all. Its preoccupation with what it likes to call 'the enlightenment project' has generally been of a distant and condescending kind, largely uninterested in the detailed political and cultural disagreements that arose between those covered by the term. By making knowledge itself the enemy of progress, this approach has closed off historical curiosity and has deprived progressive currents in contemporary political debate of a usable and honourable historical tradition upon which to build.

In this book, by contrast, I will argue that the moment of convergence between the late Enlightenment and the ideals of a republican and democratic revolution was a fundamental historical turning point. However brief its appearance, however vigorously it was thereafter repressed, it marked the beginning of all modern thought about *poverty*. Neo-conservative historiography belittles the importance of this episode in the history of social thought as little more than an eccentric tinkering with Poor Law reform. Old left historiography minimises its significance because it is still fixated upon the 'bourgeois' limitations of such programmes. Post-Marxist parlance, on the other hand, condemns it for its supposed equation between knowledge, power and emancipation, or for its imagined epistemic inadequacies on questions of race, class or gender.

What was new about this revolutionary moment at the end of the eighteenth century was the realisation that there need no longer be such thing as 'the poor'. This in turn was a product of the new conditions of the eighteenth century. After the bitter and protracted conflicts unleashed by the religious and civil wars of the sixteenth and seventeenth centuries, the eighteenth century was the first period in which the populations of many European countries experienced prolonged periods of internal peace. It was the first time, therefore, that observers were in a position to discern an underlying pattern, rhythm or system to economic life, a pattern that was relatively distinct from the bellicose politics – military, commercial and imperial – of the courts and aristocracies of Europe. This was the context in which, for the first time, contemporaries could begin to discuss the meaning and implications of living in a commercial society, or what would now be called 'capitalism'.

Across Europe, the period between the late seventeenth

and the early nineteenth centuries witnessed an increase in market-oriented activity on such a scale that economic historians have called it 'the industrious revolution'. The imperatives of commercial society reached into the poorest cottage. Leisure time declined, as the attractions of a money income or the necessity for it increased. Domestic production was increasingly devoted to marketed goods and no longer to goods or services directly consumed within the household. Seasons of under-employment in marginal agricultural areas were increasingly absorbed by spinning, weaving or other manufacturing activities in what used to be called 'the putting-out system', or more recently 'proto-industry'. There was a substantial increase in the market-oriented labour of women and children. The pace and intensity of work increased.[6]

In such a society, the afflictions regularly attending the lifecycle of wage and salary earners became clearly visible. For the first time, such afflictions could be seen to form part of a pattern which pre-existed the peculiarities of temperament or behaviour of particular individuals. This sense of a pattern was the product of a prolonged period of internal peace, of the rule of law, of growing prosperity, and of the relatively uninterrupted development of economic activity. As a result, habitual attitudes towards the poor had begun to become dislodged.

As far back as the end of the seventeenth century, the difference in prosperity between the English economy and any other in the world had been noted by John Locke. Modern

nations, even if poor in resources, could feed their populations without resort to conquest, thanks to the increasing
productivity of the land. According to Locke: 'There cannot
be a clearer demonstration than that American tribes who
possess unlimited land, but no private property, have not
one hundredth part of the Conveniences we enjoy.' A king
of one their large territories 'feeds, lodges and is clad worse
than a day labourer in England'. The same point was reiterated by Smith at the beginning of *The Wealth of Nations*.[7]

But if commercial society were associated with a progressive improvement in the conditions of life and a greater
chance of bettering one's condition, it came at a cost. The
cost of enjoying the opportunities offered by this more
volatile world was the willingness to live with chance. The
afflictions which individuals had to face were not confined
to the ups and downs of the lifecycle. There would also be
those 'constantly thrown off from the revolutions of that
wheel which no man can stop nor regulate, a number connected with commerce and adventure'.[8] The ever-changing
development of the division of labour and the expansion of
the market meant that no person's employment could be
considered wholly secure. In the nineteenth and twentieth
centuries, as the development of this market became ever
more extensive, shifts in the international division of labour
meant that thousands of families could lose their principal
source of livelihood overnight.

Finally, there was what has come to be known as 'the
vision thing', which, as most political observers are aware, is

always prone to become more expansive in times of revolution. As a result of 1776 and 1789, references to the 'people' could no longer ignore or evade questions about representation, democracy or equality, while the rich were reminded that their hegemony was provisional and contingent. Politically, the effect of the American and French Revolutions was to dislodge or undermine early modern commonplaces about the place of the poor in the social hierarchy. Instead, there emerged the beginnings of a language of social security as a basis of citizenship.

In this new approach, there was no such thing as poverty; there was no such entity as 'the poor'. In their place, there were 'a great number of individuals almost entirely dependent for the maintenance of themselves and their families either on their own labour or on the interest from capital invested so as to make their labour more productive'.[9] Such individuals encountered difficulties in the course of their lives, some predictable, some unforeseen. Some individuals were afflicted by disability from the beginning; some were disabled by accident, violence or war. Breadwinners died prematurely or became chronically sick. In old age – and now even more in extreme old age – individuals could no longer earn their living, and so were likely to need increasing amounts of care. In many instances, their families were no longer able to help them; or they might have lost what families they once had. The care of children before they were able to contribute to the livelihood of the household could also become onerous. It could be measured particularly in the temporary loss of the earnings of one of the parents, or alternatively in the cost of child care and schooling. Then again, economic misfortune might strike, not because a breadwinner died, but because marriages broke down or a partner suffered desertion. Throughout recorded history the phenomenon of the single-parent family has reappeared at the forefront of every investigation of poverty, too often to the surprise of investigators expecting to find something darker or more sinister at its unromantic core.

These new ways of thinking about the traditional notion of poverty raised new questions. Should the welfare of the poor be left to the face-to-face ministrations of the charitable, or should it be assigned to the statutory but often punitive relief afforded by the Poor Laws? Should individuals be entrusted to exercise their own independent foresight and be prepared to pit their own modest resources unaided against the uncertainties of life? Or should the development of international markets be slowed down or limited through government control or protection? Should the abandonment of leadership implied in the term *laisser faire* be condemned and replaced by a new sense of interdependence between rich and poor reminiscent of what had once supposedly pertained in the feudal world? Should people attempt to create a new sense of spiritual community? Should chance be eliminated altogether through the establishment of 'villages of cooperation' or the formation of one large 'association of the producers'? Or should governments attempt to live with chance, both national and international, but establish effective control over its effects through the universal and comprehensive adoption by their citizenry of a scheme of universal and comprehensive social insurance? As this book argues, such were the questions about poverty and its abolition which the era of the American and French Revolutions first raised – questions, or questions very like them, which are still with us today.

I

THE FRENCH REVOLUTION AND THE PROMISE OF A WORLD BEYOND WANT

It was in the 1790s at the time of the French Revolution that there first emerged the believable outlines of a world without endemic scarcity, a world in which the predictable misfortunes of life need no longer plunge the afflicted into chronic poverty or extreme want. This idea was not another version of the medieval fantasy of the land of Cockaigne, in which capons flew in through the window ready-cooked. Nor was it the update of a more serious invention, *Utopia*, most famously that created by Sir Thomas More in 1516. This was the 'nowhere', or 'good place' according to the pun contained in the Greek word, whose social customs and arrangements offered an ideal perspective from which to criticise the present and to imagine another way of being. What was put forward was neither a vision of a lost golden age nor the dream of an unreachable place; and what was described was neither a world turned upside down nor an apocalyptic community of goods.

Redistribution there would certainly be, but measured, moderate and gradual, an optimistic – but in no sense impossible – extrapolation of the progress of the century and the opportunities of the present. What were described were the new social arrangements which would underpin the peaceful land of the 'new Adam'. The French Revolution was ushering in a new world, which was spreading outwards from western Europe and the American Republic. Concretely, and in the words of English subject turned 'citizen of the world' Tom Paine, it would be a society in which 'we' no longer 'see age going to the workhouse and youth to the gallows'; one in which orphanhood, single parenthood, unemployment, sickness, old age or the loss of a breadwinner would be relieved by right.[1]

The reasons for this optimism were spelt out in general terms by the famous *philosophe* and visionary mathematician Antoine-Nicolas de Condorcet, formerly the Marquis de Condorcet, in his *Sketch for a Historical Picture of the Progress of the Human Mind*. Condorcet completed the *Sketch* while in hiding from the Jacobin authorities at the beginning of the 'Terror', on 4 October 1793. It was published by the French Republic at its own expense one year after Condorcet's death in a prison cell in March 1794, in the last months of Robespierre's rule. 'Everything tells us', Condorcet argued, 'that we are now close upon one of the great revolutions of the human race.' The intellectual progress of humankind was now about to be accompanied by a material transformation of the human condition. 'The labours of recent ages', Condorcet wrote, 'have done much for the honour of man, something for his liberty, but so far almost nothing for his happiness.'[2] But the history of modern times – from Descartes to the French Revolution – had prepared the way for a great change in the physical and social prospects of mankind. This transformation had already begun. Condorcet attempted to describe its trajectory in his concluding chapter of the *Sketch*, 'The Future Progress of the Human Mind'.

Against those who maintained that the gulf between rich and poor was an inescapable part of 'civilisation', Condorcet argued that inequality was largely to be ascribed to 'the present imperfections of the social art'. 'The final end of the social art' would be 'real equality' – 'the abolition of inequality between nations' and 'the progress of equality within each nation'. Ultimately, this progress would lead to 'the true perfection of mankind'. Apart from the 'natural differences between men', the only kind of inequality to persist would be 'that which is in the interests of all and which favours the progress of civilisation, of education and of industry, without entailing either poverty, humiliation or dependence'. That would be in a world in which 'everyone will have the knowledge necessary to conduct himself in the ordinary affairs of life, according to the light of his own reason', where 'everyone will become able, through the development of his faculties, to find the means of providing for his needs'; and where, at last, 'misery and folly will be the exception, and no longer the habitual lot of a section of society'.[3]

Beyond France, slavery would be abolished, colonies would become independent and commerce would spread worldwide under the aegis of free trade. Asia and Africa would break free from 'our trade monopolies, our treachery, our murderous contempt for men of another colour or creed, the insolence of our usurpations'; they would no longer be prey to 'the shameful superstition' brought to these peoples by monks. Instead, assistance would be provided by men occupied in 'teaching them about their interests and their rights'. Soon, large tribes would become civilised and races so long oppressed by 'sacred despots or dull-witted conquerors' would gain their freedom. Eventually, even savage tribes and 'conquering hordes who know no other law but force' would merge into 'civilised nations'.[4]

This vision of a new international order would have been shared by many different strands of progressive opinion in the last decades of the eighteenth century. The horrors of the slave trade and the shame of colonialism had become well-known topics of debate in the aftermath of the Seven Years War in the oft-cited writings of Montesquieu, the Quakers, Abbé Raynal and Adam Smith in the 1760s and 1770s.[5]

Far more novel and distinctive were the proposals set out in the *Sketch* to forward 'the progress of equality within each nation'. In the agriculture and industry of the 'enlightened nations' of Europe, Condorcet pointed out, 'a great number of individuals' were almost entirely dependent for the maintenance of themselves and their family 'either on their own labour or on the interest from capital invested so as to make their labour more productive'. In contrast to those owning land or capital, these groups depended directly 'on the life and even on the health of the head of the family'. Their livelihood was 'rather like a life annuity, save that it is more dependent on chance'. 'Here then', wrote Condorcet, 'is a necessary cause of inequality, of dependence and even of misery, which ceaselessly threatens the most numerous and most active class in our society.'[6]

But such inequality could be 'in great part eradicated'. People in old age could be guaranteed a means of livelihood 'produced partly by their own savings and partly by the savings of others who make the same outlay, but who die before they need to reap the reward'. A similar principle of compensation could be applied by securing for widows and orphans 'an income which is the same and costs the same for those families which suffer an early loss and for those who suffer it later'. Through the application of the same principle, it would also be possible to provide all children with the capital necessary for the full use of their labour at the age when they started work and founded a family.[7]

In Condorcet's conception, the necessary complement to these proposals was a universal scheme of education. The aim was not only to enable the citizen to 'manage his household, administer his affairs and employ his labour and faculties in freedom', but also to 'know his rights and be able to exercise them'; and even beyond that, to 'be a stranger to none of the high and delicate feelings which honour human nature'. The priority was to avoid all 'dependence, whether forced or voluntary'. In his 1791 proposals for a national education system in France, Condorcet had underlined the same theme: 'it is impossible for instruction, even when equal, not to increase the superiority of those whom nature has endowed more favourably. But to maintain equality of rights, it is enough that this superiority entail no real dependence: that each individual be sufficiently instructed to exercise for himself the right guaranteed him under the law, without subjecting himself blindly to the reason of another.'[8]

The danger of dependence, whether economic or spiritual, was not confined to the use of patronage by rich and powerful individuals or by corporations. It extended equally to government. For that reason, public education instituted by government must be limited to instruction. The teaching of the constitution of each nation should 'only form part of instruction as a matter of fact'. The danger of any other approach was that public education might be identified with the inculcation of 'a kind of political religion', and that the citizen might become attached to the constitution 'by a blind sentiment'. Such measures often went together with a yearning to return to the patriotic ethos of the ancient republic, ignoring the fact that 'the aim of education can no longer be to consecrate established opinions, but, on the contrary, to subject them to free examination by succeeding generations that will be progressively more enlightened'.[9]

The practical application of such a scheme in England, in the shape of a detailed set of proposals to replace the Poor Rate by a tax-based system of universal insurance, was set forth in the second part of Tom Paine's *Rights of Man*, published in February 1792. A more redistributory variant of the same idea was argued in his later pamphlet *Agrarian Justice*, which appeared in England in 1797.

Paine put forward his proposals as part of a larger reformation in the practice of government which would follow the replacement of monarchy by a representative and democratic republic. In England, he claimed, there were 'two distinct characters of government'. There was first a 'civil government or the government of laws which operates at home' and was composed of a set of institutions 'attended with little charge' since the country 'administers and executes them, at its own expense by means of magistrates, juries, sessions, and assize, over and above the taxes which it pays'. On the other hand, there was 'court or cabinet government which operates abroad, on the rude plan of uncivilised life', and was attended with 'boundless extravagance'.[10]

In England under monarchical government, Paine claimed, 'every war terminates with an addition of taxes'; 'taxes were not raised to carry on wars, but wars were raised to carry on taxes'. Parliamentary government had been 'the most productive machine of taxation ever invented'. Yet 'not a thirtieth, scarcely a fortieth part of the taxes which are raised in England are either occasioned by, or applied to the purpose of civil government'. This was why Paine believed that 'the hordes of miserable poor with which old countries abound' were 'the consequence of what in such countries they call government'. 'In the present state of things,' Paine wrote, 'a labouring man with a wife or two or three children does not pay less than between seven and eight pounds a year in taxes.' The labourer was not aware of this since it was concealed from him in the articles he bought and he therefore complained only of their dearness. But since these hidden taxes amounted to at least 'a fourth part of his yearly earnings', he was 'consequently disabled from providing for a family, especially if himself, or any of them, are afflicted with sickness'. [11]

This reasoning provided the justification for Paine's proposals. Relying on Sir John Sinclair's *History of the Revenue*, he estimated that since 1714 it had cost £70 million to maintain the Hanoverian monarchy – 'a family imported from abroad'. If courtly sinecures were abolished and no office holder were to receive a salary in excess of £10,000, Paine estimated that together with the necessary defence costs of a peacetime establishment, £1.5 million per year would be sufficient to maintain 'the honest purposes of government'. This would leave a surplus of more than £6 million revenue. The use of this surplus to remove or alleviate the most obvious precipitants of chronic want would also make it possible to abolish the major form of additional local taxation, the Poor Rate, 'a direct tax' amounting to £2 million per year, 'which every householder feels and who knows also to the last farthing'.

Paine identified the two most pressing forms of poverty as 'the expense of bringing up children' in large families, and the diminution of strength and employability in old age. He therefore proposed that a grant of £4 per annum be made to every child under fourteen, and pensions of £6 per annum to all over fifty, rising to £10 per annum for those of sixty and over. Like Condorcet, however, he also stressed the centrality of education to any scheme of social amelioration. The £4 per annum was to be spent on sending children to school to learn 'reading, writing and common arithmetic', their attendance to be certified by ministers in every parish. The reasons for this were as much political as social. 'A nation under a well-regulated government should permit none to remain uninstructed. It is monarchical and aristocratical government only that requires ignorance for its support.'

Paine also attempted to remedy the poverty trap which his scheme might cause. There were, he noted, 'a number of families who, though not properly of the class of poor, yet find it difficult to give education to their children; and such children, under such a case, would be in a worse condition than if their parents were actually poor'. Supposing there to be 400,000 such children, he proposed that each of these be allowed 10s. per annum for six years, which would give them six months' schooling a year and 'half a crown for paper and spelling books'.[12]

Paine completed his scheme with a number of smaller grants: 20s. to be given 'immediately on the birth of a child to every woman who should make the demand'; and similarly 20s. to every newly married couple. Grants should be made available to defray the funeral expenses of those 'who, travelling for work, may die at a distance from their friends'. Shelter and employment should be provided to those young and without skill or connections – 'the casual poor' – migrating to London and especially liable to fall into distress. Allowances should be made to soldiers and sailors disbanded as a result of the new state of peace, with increases of pay for those who remained, along with other deserving low-income groups, such as curates and 'inferior revenue officers' – a category to which Paine himself had once belonged.[13]

As Paine summed up the effects of his plan:

> The poor laws, those instruments of civil torture, will be superceded, and the wasteful expense of litigation prevented. The hearts of the humane will not be shocked by ragged and hungry children, and persons of seventy and eighty years of age, begging for bread. The dying poor will not be dragged from place to place to breathe their last, as a reprisal of parish upon parish. Widows will have a maintenance for their children, and not be carted away on the death of their husbands, like culprits and criminals; and children will no longer be considered as increasing the distresses of their parents. The haunts of the wretched will be known, because it will be to their advantage; and the number of petty crimes, the offspring of distress and poverty, will be lessened. The poor, as well as the rich, will then be interested in the support of government, and the cause and apprehension of riots and tumults will cease.[14]

The proposals of Condorcet and those of Paine bear some clear and unmistakable similarities, not only in specific points of emphasis, but in a shared optimism about the role of knowledge, reason and freedom in the overcoming of poverty, violence and ignorance. The immediate reason for this affinity is clear enough. It arose from the collaboration between the two men in the increasingly fevered and frightening political battles fought out in revolutionary France, from the move towards a republic following the king's attempted flight and capture at Varennes on 21 June 1791 to the expulsion from the Convention and arrest of Girondin deputies, with whom both Condorcet and Paine were associated, on 2 June 1793.[15]

But the affinity between their positions also had deeper roots. For both men subscribed to a new form of republicanism, forged out of three major political and intellectual developments in the last third of the eighteenth century. The first was a more confident belief in the control over chance and the future through the coming together of the collection of vital statistics and the mathematics of probability. The second was the great impetus given to the growth of positive future-oriented conceptions of commercial society following the publication of Adam Smith's *Wealth of Nations* in 1776, and in France the liberal reforms attempted by the Turgot ministry of 1774–6. The third was the radicalisation of the understanding of each of these starting points under the impact of the American and French Revolutions.

The first of these developments concerned what Condorcet described as 'the calculus of probabilities'. Condorcet based his confidence in the future upon the possibilities opened up by this 'calculus' in all forms of knowledge. Back in 1782, at the time of his appointment as permanent secretary to the Academy of Sciences, Condorcet had stressed the importance of this calculus, both as the basis of the connection between scientific and social advance and as the common foundation of the moral and physical sciences, which henceforth 'must follow the same methods, acquire an equally exact and precise language, attain the same degree of certainty'. [16] Condorcet had come to share David Hume's belief that all truths, even mathematical truths, were no more than probable. But this was in no sense a concession to scepticism. Like Hume, Condorcet did not doubt the reality of necessity, only the possibility of our knowing it. In the moral sciences, the recognition of all truths as in different degrees probable would allow the introduction of precision into the knowledge of human affairs in place of the 'prejudices planted by superstition and tyranny'.

More ambitiously, a probabilistic approach would make possible a single mathematically based social science, or what Condorcet came to call 'social mathematics'. The most contentious part of this new science was its theory of rationality – half descriptive and half prescriptive – which was to be applied to all processes of human decision-making. Like the putative agent depicted by twentieth-century games theorists or proponents of 'rational choice', rational man would act to maximise his interest according to the balance of probabilities. Ultimately, if every individual were enabled to think rationally, the conflict between individual and common interest would disappear and all would acknowledge 'the sweet despotism of reason'. This emphasis upon the reformation of mental processes helps to explain the importance attached to instruction in Condorcet's educational reforms. The centrality of mental reform to the security and harmonious operation of the new French Republic was reiterated by Condorcet's followers among the Idéologues, the group led by Destutt de Tracy and Cabanis in the class of moral sciences at the newly founded Institut (intended as a 'living encyclopedia') in France under the Directorate between 1795 and 1801. It was also echoed to some extent by Bentham and his circle in Britain.

But such problems did not arise so directly in the area of what might be called social insurance. Here it was more a question of transforming a variety of existing but partial practices into a framework which would be truly comprehensive. In the *Sketch*, Condorcet included among existing applications of 'the calculus of probability', 'the organisation of life annuities, tontines, private savings, benefit schemes and insurance policies of every kind'.[17] Successful forms of 'the application of the calculus to the probabilities of life and the investment of money' now existed. But in the coming epoch, as a means of reducing inequality, they should be applied 'in a sufficiently comprehensive and exhaustive fashion to render them really useful, not merely to a few individuals, but to society as a whole, by making it possible to prevent those periodic disasters which strike at so many families and which are such a recurrent source of misery and suffering'.[18]

Paine's days as an excise man may have left him with a sharpened knowledge of the operation of the tax system, but he did not possess expert knowledge in either mathematics or statistics. Nevertheless, his proposals were based upon similar assumptions. He justified his pension scheme as a *right* rather than a charity, with estimates of the tax the recipients would have paid during their working lives. 'Converting, therefore, his (or her) individual tax in a tontine, the money he shall receive after fifty years is but little more than the legal interest of the nett money he has paid.'[19]

Later, in *Agrarian Justice*, published in 1797, Paine proposed grants of £15 for all 21-year-olds and annual pensions of £10 for those over fifty, to be paid out of a national fund collected from death duties on estates and fortunes above a certain size. Justifying the roughness of his actuarial assumptions, he explained that 'my state of health prevents my making sufficient inquiries with respect to the doctrine of probabilities, whereon to found calculations with such degrees of certainty, as they are capable of'. Defending his scheme as an alternative to charity, he argued that there was 'but little any individual can do, when the whole extent of the misery to be relieved is considered'. It was 'only by organising civilisation upon such principles as to act like a system of pullies that the whole weight of misery can be removed'.[20]

Social insurance of the kind proposed by Condorcet involved the application of the mathematics of probability to questions of life expectancy on the basis of mortality statistics. But the coming together of the apparently self-evident set of procedures presupposed in Condorcet's proposal was less straightforward than it might first appear. Until around 1750, each of the components combined in social insurance had developed in relative isolation. Pioneering work in the mathematics of probability had been done by Pascal, Fermat, Huygens and De Witt in the mid-seventeenth century. But the problems considered were those encountered in lotteries, coin-tossing and games of chance. They were not immediately related to the concerns of 'political arithmetic', in which questions of life expectancy and its measurement by means of mortality statistics were eventually encountered.

Bills of mortality had been recorded in London parishes since 1562, not because of any civic interest in life expectancy, but in order to provide an early warning of the onset of plague. The first analyst of these tables to speculate about the relationship between age and death was John Graunt, whose *Natural and Political Observations on the Bills of Mortality* appeared in 1662. But his main interest was again in immediate policy issues, for example, the number of able-bodied males available for military service and the limited effect of quarantine as a means of containing the spread of plague. His tables assumed that for the average English person, after the age of six there was an equal chance of dying in any of the seven decades that followed. This lack of interest in the empirical details of age at death was highlighted by the fact that, while cause and place of death were recorded, age at death was not included in the bills of mortality until 1728. Even in the case of the pricing of annuities, a procedure in which states had an obvious interest since annuities were sold as a means of servicing debt, a system of estimating life expectancy based upon relevant empirical information was slow to develop. The first proposal to use probability theory in order to price annuities was that made by Jan de Witt to the Estates General of Holland and West Friesland in 1671. He estimated probability of death as a correlate of age, but did not employ statistics and simply assumed that the risk of death remained the same for all ages between three and fifty-three.[21]

The problem was as much political as intellectual. Sharp and mathematically trained observers soon saw how mortality statistics could extend mathematical probability beyond games of chance. In a memorandum of 1700, Leibniz suggested measurements of life expectancy, age distribution and geographical distribution of disease and causes of death.[22] By the 1720s, mathematicians like De Moivre had produced life tables as a simplified guide to the pricing of annuities. Yet despite their common interest in the sale of annuities either as business or as a means of servicing debt repayment, neither insurance companies nor governments paid much attention to the advantages of applying the calculus of probabilities to reliable series of statistics until the middle of the eighteenth century.

In the case of the insurance industry, Keith Thomas and other historians have taken its appearance in London towards the end of the seventeenth century as evidence of the emergence of new attitudes towards control of the future and the minimisation of the consequences of unavoidable risk. But this was only half true. The period between the 1690s and the 1740s was chiefly notable for a succession of speculative manias and 'bubbles' in which insurance schemes figured almost as prominently as John Law's plan for the reflation of France and the South Sea Bubble. Insurance policies were placed alongside annuities and lottery tickets, while the law reinforced the association between insurance and gambling by grouping them together in a common notion of risk.

As Lorraine Daston has argued, the obstacles to the development of a modern conception of life insurance were first and foremost social. It was not until there emerged a new attitude towards the welfare of the family within the professions and the middling ranks – clergy, doctors, lawyers, skilled artisans – that there could develop a form of life insurance based upon mathematical probability and reliable series of statistics. This new attitude valued predictability and prudence above luck, and provision for the family above provision for self. In place of the desire for speculative winnings, which had been the motivation behind tontines and lotteries, the new insurance ethos was governed by the fear of downward social mobility occasioned by death or bankruptcy. Its promise was that 'a man who is rich today will not be poor tomorrow'.[23]

The emergence of these new attitudes was signalled by the unprecedented success of The Society for Equitable Insurance on Lives and Survivorships, founded in 1762. The effective founder of this society was the mathematician James Dodson, who calculated premiums on the basis of the London bills of mortality. This marked a radical break with contemporary practice, in which premiums were set more by guesswork than by tables. It also transformed the position of the actuary, who until then had acted as no more than a secretary and book-keeper, and was without mathematical skills. The novelty of the enterprise was underlined by the grounds given by the Privy Council for rejecting the first application to form the society in 1761. It doubted the mathematical process by which 'the chance of mortality is attempted to be reduced to a certain standard: this is a mere speculation, never yet tried in practice'.[24]

Government interest in the collection of statistics in the seventeenth and eighteenth centuries was in nearly every case driven by military or fiscal needs. This is also partly why social insurance came to be of interest to the French state in the 1780s and after. At the end of the American War of Independence in 1783, the French government became increasingly anxious to extend its tax base. But in the absence of significant tax reform, governments were forced to continue to rely upon lotteries and life annuity contracts to cover the gap between expenditure and tax revenue. The pricing of such expedients demanded precise probabilistic skills and accurate mortality data. In this situation, Condorcet's theoretical vision of the calculus of probabilities suddenly acquired a pressing practical relevance. Politically engaged mathematicians and scientists, pre-eminently Condorcet and Lavoisier, were able to exert influence on government policy and practice. In the 1780s the Academy of Sciences decided to print the population statistics which had been demanded annually from the intendants from 1772 and further to establish a public bureau of statistics as a department of the National Treasury.

At the same time, the success of the Society for Equitable Insurance in Britain had begun to attract a host of French imitators. This was also of financial interest to the government, which regarded its insurance monopoly as another lucrative source of income. From the mid 1780s, there were numerous schemes of social insurance proposed, some primarily humanitarian, others purely speculative. Once again, Condorcet, together with Lavoisier, Laplace and others, often sat on committees appointed by the Academy of Sciences to assess such schemes. Particularly important were the contributions made by Duvillard de Durand.

Like Condorcet himself, Duvillard had gained his first political experience, as a junior civil servant in the Controller-General's office, in the 1774–6 reforming ministry of Condorcet's hero, Turgot. Thereafter he worked in the Treasury and later in the statistical bureau of the Ministry of the Interior. In 1786, he impressed the Academy of Sciences with a report on debt and annuities. In 1788, he acted as the 'profound mathematician' in the employ of the French Compagnie Royale d'Assurance, modelled explicitly on the English Equitable Society, in its victorious bid for the insurance monopoly. Together with Condorcet and other members of the *ancien règime* liberal élite, Duvillard was a member of the Society of 1789 whose official aims were to develop 'the social art' and to apply its principles to the establishment of a new constitution. Other members of this exclusive and sometimes self-consciously elitist society included Lafayette, the duc de La Rochefoucauld (-d'Enville), the duc de La Rochefoucauld-Liancourt and Dupont de Nemours and later Sieyès – all, apart from Sieyès, old allies of Condorcet. It was the Comité de Mendicité, appointed by the National Assembly and headed by the duc de La Rochefoucauld, that invited Duvillard to draw up a national plan for life insurance, the *Plan d'une association de prévoyance*. Of the three mathematicians appointed by the Academy of Sciences to review this plan, two – Condorcet and Vandermonde – were members of the Society of 1789.

But Condorcet did not merely vet or puff the schemes of others, he also put forward proposals of his own. One of his schemes was occasioned by a plan proposed in 1785 by André Jean de Larocque which suggested the establishment of a general savings fund into which working people invested regular amounts in return for annuities which would secure them against premature retirement or old age. Both Lavoisier and Condorcet proposed variants of this scheme. In 1790 Condorcet proposed 'accumulating funds' (*caisses d'accumulation*) which would both serve as a form of government borrowing and release funds for general investment by removing the need to hoard against the possibility of misfortune. The *caisses d'accumulation* would also create what Condorcet later described in the *Sketch* as 'a rich, active, populous nation without the existence of a poor corrupted class'.[25]

The radicalism of Condorcet and Paine was also distinctive in a second sense. It was a radicalism built upon the emancipatory possibilities of commercial society, as they had been elaborated in the works and proposals for reform of Adam Smith and Turgot. There were clear differences, however, in the philosophical assumptions which inspired these two thinkers. Turgot believed that citizens had rights which 'exist independently of society' and 'form its necessary elements'. He was also a rationalist who believed that the process of decision-making in public assemblies should be designed not merely to produce expressions of political will but to act as a vehicle for the discovery of truth. He was a strong advocate of universal education, not simply as an answer to the ever-shifting character of the demand for skills attending the development of the division of labour, but as a way of inculcating a civic spirit among the citizenry. He also believed in the perfectibility of the human species.[26]

By contrast, Smith avoided discussion of rights which he associated with Locke and opted for a markedly more

minimalist account of the political preconditions of a functioning commercial state. He wrote in 1755: '[L]ittle else is
requisite to carry a state to the highest degree of opulence
from the lowest barbarism, but peace, easy taxes and a tol-
erable administration of justice.'[27] He followed Hume in
rejecting a contractarian account of the origins of government. Political obligation did not derive from a contract,
but was the result of either natural deference to established
authority or a regard for 'common or general interest' or
'public utility'. Similarly, Smith was not a rationalist. 'The
natural progress of opulence' had been brought about,
not because reason had played an ever-increasing part in
human affairs, but because the vanity of feudal lords had led
them to barter away their retainers in exchange for 'baubles
and trinkets'. The delusion that wealth and power would
bring happiness 'keeps in continual motion the industry of
mankind'.[28]

Finally, Smith had no faith in the perfectibility of
mankind. On the contrary, he became increasingly fearful
of the possibility of an attempt at wholesale reform by a
doctrinaire 'man of system'. For, however much he cherished the fact that 'the lowest and most despised member
of civilised society' enjoyed 'superior affluence and abundance' when compared with 'the most respected and active
savage', it remained the case that 'laws and government may
be considered … as a combination of the rich to oppress
the poor and to preserve to themselves the inequality of
goods which would otherwise be soon destroyed by the

attacks of the poor'.[29] Deference and admiration for the rich kept an exchange society in motion, but it was a fragile construction. Therefore, despite his wholehearted praise for the growing moral and political independence of members of commercial society, Smith's account was never free from an undertow of unease: a nervous dread about what would happen if it became true, as Paine claimed in 1797, that 'the superstitious awe, the enslaving reverence that formerly surrounded affluence is passing away in all countries leaving the possessor of property to the convulsion of accidents'.[30]

Neither Turgot nor Condorcet could have felt comfortable with a theory of history which placed so much weight upon unintended consequences. Turgot earlier in his career had appeared to believe that history was a sort of theodicy in which evil was compelled to contribute towards the progress of the good: but as a reformer, he considered that the source of bad customs was bad laws. Without a residue of Christian belief to defend, Condorcet believed straightforwardly that all moral and political errors were the result of philosophical errors.[31] But these convictions did not pose an obstacle to their common acceptance of the basic premiss of Smith's 'science of the legislator': that the well-being of a state was commensurate with the well-being of the individuals who composed it; that most regulation only benefited privileged groups; and that the surest advice to 'the legislator' was to trust to our common 'desire of bettering our condition'.[32] From this shared starting point, Smith and Turgot drew similar practical conclusions. According to

Dugald Stewart, writing in 1793–4 about Smith's encounters with Turgot in Paris in 1765–6, 'the satisfaction he enjoyed in the conversation of Turgot may easily be imagined. Their opinions on the most essential points of political economy were the same; and they were both animated by the same zeal for the best interests of mankind.'[33]

This closeness of outlook was reproduced in the arguments of Condorcet and Paine. Condorcet remained a political disciple of Turgot. Fêted as a mathematician from his twenties, Condorcet, like Laplace, became a protégé of the mathematician and editor of the *Encyclopedia* D'Alembert. It was through D'Alembert that he was admitted to the Academy of Sciences and introduced to the salon of Mlle Lespinasse, where he met Turgot. He assisted in Turgot's reforming ministry of 1774–6 and remained in constant correspondence with the ex-Controller General after his fall. When Turgot died, he wrote an admiring study, *Vie de Monsieur Turgot*, in 1783.

Like Smith and Turgot, Condorcet was an enthusiast for free trade, on the grounds that 'the natural tendency' of wealth to equality would be enhanced if 'free trade and industry were allowed to remove the advantages that accrued wealth derives from any restrictive law or fiscal privilege'.[34] On the question of education, however, it was the ideas of Turgot, and before him the Physiocrats, which were to the fore. In the *Memoire sur les municipalités* (drafted by Dupont de Nemours in 1775 as a digest of Turgot's ideas and intended as a submission to the young Louis XVI), it was proposed that a national educational council be set up to direct public instruction according to uniform principles. The aim would be to produce a more enlightened citizenry 'submitting to authority not from fear but through reason'.[35] Many of these ideas reappeared in more radical and less authoritarian form in Condorcet's proposals for public instruction in 1791–2. The aim was that 'each individual be sufficiently instructed to exercise for himself the rights guaranteed him under the law, without subjecting himself blindly to the reason of another'.[36]

Condorcet followed Smith in remarking that the more mechanical occupations became, 'the greater the danger that the people will contract that stupidity which is natural to men limited to a small number of ideas, all of the same kind'. 'Instruction' in place of apprenticeship was the only remedy for this evil, 'which is all the more dangerous in a state to the extent that the laws have established greater equality'.[37] But it was also in this context that the programmes of Turgot and Smith diverged. In one of his few explicit criticisms, Condorcet criticised Smith's proposal that public regulation and financial support should leave instruction itself to a competition between different churches. Condorcet explained this as a rare lapse in the exactitude and precision which governed the rest of Smith's work.[38] Condorcet wished to exclude the church from education, not for specifically anti-Christian reasons, but for the same reason that Turgot had already put to Louis XVI in 1776: 'Your kingdom, Sire, is of this world. The purpose of education, therefore, was to fit the citizen for his rights and duties as a member of civil society'.[39]

In the case of Paine, evidence of an acquaintance with Smith and enthusiasm about the future of commercial society is scattered plentifully throughout his writings. Paine in *Rights of Man: Part One*, contrasted 'the disorderly cast' of Burke's argument compared with Smith's reasoning 'from minutiae to magnitude'. He clearly built some of his picture both of the power of the feudal barony as the result of conquest in English history and of 'the progress which the peaceful arts of agriculture, manufacture and commerce have made beneath such a long accumulating load of discouragement and oppression' from a reading of Book Three of *The Wealth of Nations*.[40] More specifically, Paine's proposals of progressive taxation in *Rights of Man: Part Two*, and of death duties in *Agrarian Justice* as a means of combating entails and primogeniture, if not actually advocated in Smith, were quite in the spirit of Smith's criticism: '[T]hey are founded upon the most absurd of all suppositions, the supposition that every successive generation of men have not an equal right to the earth and all that it possesses; but that the property of the present generation should be restrained and regulated according to the fancy of those who died perhaps five hundred years ago.'[41] So much for Burke's appeal to the principle of prescription!

What is also striking, however, is the meticulous way in which Paine distinguished his own case for 'agrarian justice' from the many theories of 'agrarian law', from Spence to

Babeuf, resting on an appeal to a primitive right to the earth in common. 'Nothing could be more unjust than Agrarian Law in a country improved by cultivation.' Paine proposed a tax in the form of a 'ground rent' to be paid as recompense for the loss to the community of access to the land in its original unimproved state. But, as he recognised, 'it is never possible to go from the civilised to the natural state' since 'man in a natural state, subsisting by hunting' would have required 'ten times the quantity of land to range over to procure himself sustenance, than would support him in a civilised state, where the earth is cultivated'.[42]

Starting from a future-oriented theory of commercial society, this distinctively modern form of radicalism enjoyed a number of advantages. Not the least important was the way in which it enabled Condorcet and Paine to get beyond the repetitive terms of the eighteenth-century debate about luxury and poverty, virtue and self-interest. In a passage not finally included in the *Sketch*, Condorcet associated the pursuit of 'superfluities' both with the progress of commercial society and with intellectual advance. He wrote of 'that need for ideas and new feelings which is the prime mover in the progress of the human mind ... that taste for the superfluities of luxury which is the spur of industry' and 'that spirit of curiosity which eagerly penetrates the veil nature has drawn across her secrets'. In his 1791 essay on 'Public Instruction', he stated that from the perspective of 'the equality of wellbeing', it was 'irrelevant to the general happiness that a few men enjoy more elaborate pleasures as a result of their wealth provided that men can satisfy their needs with facility, attaining in their housing, their dress, their food, in all the habits of their daily life, a measure of health and cleanliness, and even of comfort and attractiveness'. He favoured simpler manners, but not as the product of 'misguided notions of austerity'. As for self-interest, it was only a problem if viewed statically. In the future, the perfection of laws and public institutions, consequent upon the progress of the sciences, would accomplish 'the reconciliation, the identification of the interests of each with the interests of all'.[44]

Paine was equally confident that reform did not require moral improvement. 'As to the mere theoretical reformation, I have never preached it up. The most effectual process is that of improving the condition of man by means of his interest.' He believed this to be possible because 'all the great laws of society are laws of nature. Those of trade and commerce, whether with respect to the intercourse of individuals or of nations, are laws of mutual and reciprocal interest. They are followed and obeyed, because it is the interest of the parties so to do'; and in an aside similar to Condorcet, he stated, 'I care not how affluent some may be, providing none are miserable in consequence of it.' Indeed, in a neat challenge to the conventional understanding of asceticism which informed government and radicals alike, he wrote, 'I know not why any plant or herb of the field should be a greater luxury in one country than another.' But 'an overgrown estate in either is a luxury at all times, and, as such, is the proper object of taxation'.[45]

This removal of moral opprobrium from the language of 'luxury' was not characteristic of most forms of radicalism. Until the publication of *The Wealth of Nations*, it was difficult to disentangle the notion of a polity based upon moderate gradations of wealth from the idea of an austere and virtuous republic. The terms of the debate had been set at the beginning of the eighteenth century in the writings of Fénelon and Mandeville.[46] *The Adventures of Telemachus, Son of Ulysses* by Archbishop Fénelon, the famous critic of the last years of Louis XIV, was published in 1699, translated almost immediately into English and became one of the most popular and reprinted books of the century. Even at the end of the eighteenth century, William Godwin claimed that the just man should rescue Fénelon from the flames in preference to his own brother or father.[47] In Fénelon's critique, 'luxury' had been associated with the extremes of inequality. The book described how Telemachus, under the guidance of a disguised Minerva, had learnt the art of virtuous kingship. His reform of Salentum (France) depicted a programme for growth without luxury. Foreign trade would be restricted to a single and highly regulated port, sumptuary laws would eliminate the craving for 'superfluities', manufacture would be restricted to 'real' needs and urban workers in the luxury trades would be resettled on the land.

Mandeville's response, *The Fable of the Bees* of 1714, was a defence of the existing commercial economy of Orange and Hanoverian England against Fénelon's neo-Jacobite appeal. It pointed out that 'luxury' or 'superfluities' were not confined to the rich, but was only an invidious way of describing the new needs which developed with civilisation itself: a constant development in which what was first thought 'superfluous' soon became 'necessary'. The more contentious part of his message was directed at the hypocrisy of the language in which commercial society was defended. Mandeville maintained that morality and justice were simply devices of the rich to deceive the poor. The Christian values which supposedly underpinned society were a mere façade. Mankind could not be governed by reason and sympathy, only by flattery and deceit. If Christian moderation or self-denial were really to triumph, as pious apologias professed to desire, the result would be a more equal, but much poorer society, since equality and poverty went together. The paradox of a commercial society was that private vices – the incessant quest for luxury and love of display, an entirely self-regarding though hypocritically veiled self-interest – produced public virtue, a dynamic and innovative economy which kept the poor in constant employment.

In at least two respects, the terms of this debate help to explain Smith's importance in shaping the subsequent radicalism of Condorcet and Paine. Firstly, if a new form of radicalism were to be possible, there had to be something else between the agrarian austerity of Salentum and the selfish free-for-all celebrated by Mandeville. Secondly, no form of radicalism could tolerate the position of the rich if all they were supposed to do was engage in conspicuous consumption and spendthrift hedonism.

On the first point, what had made Mandeville's depiction of commercial society so unappetising was his denial (following Hobbes) that sociability was natural to man. This meant that justice and morality were no more than the inventions of 'skilful politicians'. Smith denied that society was simply built upon this form of individualism. Although vanity and delusion in man's nature could not be denied, human desire for betterment was not solely displayed in naked self-interest. Man did not merely love praise, he was capable of actions which were praiseworthy. Through language, man was endowed with a capacity for mutual sympathy and understanding. This capacity to put oneself in the place of another elaborated into the idea of an 'impartial spectator' formed the basis of Smith's theory of 'moral sentiment'. The impartial spectator, 'the man within the breast', was a shorthand for the way in which the judgement of others became interiorised within the self and acted as a constant check upon the unqualified egoism which might otherwise prevail. The value of this idea as a way of getting beyond the antinomies presented by Fénelon and Mandeville became apparent during the French Revolution. The radical search for some alternative to Christian ethics or ancient republicanism led to the translation of Smith's *Theory of Moral Sentiments* in 1798 by Sophie de Grouchy, Condorcet's widow.[48]

The second point highlights Smith's relevance to changing eighteenth-century attitudes towards chance. The logic of Mandeville's anti-ascetic argument led him to praise all forms of conspicuous consumption provided only that expenditure occurred within the confines of the domestic economy. Somewhat perversely, this now meant that the spendthrift became hero and that the unbridled gambling of the South Sea Bubble era appeared to acquire a solid economic justification. One of the most important advances made by *The Wealth of Nations* was to demonstrate that, while the employment-generating function of the consumption of the rich still needed to be acknowledged, the longer term progress of an exchange economy was dependent upon something more solid than prodigal expenditure. From his Paris visit of 1763–4, Smith learnt to distinguish between 'unproductive labour' – that used up in consumption and display – and 'useful and productive labour', which was the product of investment and the true measure of a nation's wealth. The development of the division of labour depended upon capital accumulation and capital accumulation depended on investment.[49]

Deferral of immediate consumption was therefore not mere miserliness, but evidence of an aspiration to treat the future as something other than the capricious goddess Fortuna of Renaissance statesmen or the dazzling uncertainties of the eighteenth-century gaming table. Just as the associations of insurance began to shift in the 1760s, an analogous change occurred in conceptions of commercial society, highlighted by the crucial position now accorded to investment in Smith's conception of the economy as a whole. By the 1780s, links between these changes were becoming more common. One example in France, an inspiration of Condorcet's suggested *caisses d'accumulation* in 1790, was André Larocque's 1785 proposal for a *caisse générale des épargnes du peuple*, which would invest funds formed by regular contributions by working people and return the proceeds in the form of annuities to be paid out in old age or as a consequence of early retirement.

∽

The arrival of new ideas about the control over chance and new future-oriented conceptions of commercial society in the 1760s and 1770s, which provided some of the pre-conditions for the new radicalism, may help to explain the shape of Condorcet's and Paine's interest in insurance. What this does not explain, however, is the comprehensive national scope of these schemes and the radicalism of the redistribution of income which would underpin them.

On the question of social insurance, the uniqueness of Paine's proposals can be highlighted by comparing them with those of another radical and one-time partial mentor of Paine, the famous Welsh dissenting preacher Richard Price. Price was, among his other accomplishments, a distinguished mathematician and pioneer of social insurance. After Philip Dodson's death, he had been called in to help the Equitable Society and had selected a new series of mortality tables based on Northampton and calculated the Society's premiums. He remained the Society's actuarial expert until he passed over the position to his nephew in 1782. Price and Paine had been closely allied on the American question and Price may have been responsible for Paine's belief that poverty in civilised countries was increasing. But from the 1770s to the 1790s there was a growing divergence between their views on the future of commercial society. Price's view of the economy remained close to that of Fénelon, and to the English commonwealth tradition. He was therefore little affected by Smith, who considered Price to be a poor calculator and a 'most superficial philosopher'.

Price thought not only that poverty was increasing, but that population was declining, that only certain forms of commerce were compatible with virtue, and that luxury was enervating the nation. His advice to the Americans was to avoid foreign trade and luxury. Finally, and most importantly, his view of the poor was moralistic and conventional. Although he backed various parliamentary proposals for social insurance, notably those of Masères in 1773 and Acland in 1786, these schemes were not comprehensive, nor did they replace the Poor Rate system or contain any redistributory component.[50] His proposals did not look forward to twentieth-century schemes of social insurance, but rather to the mid-Victorian Gladstonian legislation promoting provident savings banks.

There was also an equally clear gap between Smith's approach to the question of equality and the radical use of his writings to justify the reduction of inequality by directly political means. The whole point of Smith's famous sentence about 'the invisible hand' when it was introduced into his

Theory of Moral Sentiments was that, although commercial society perpetuated and reinforced inequality, it also just as consistently mitigated its effects by the ways in which it channelled the expenditure of the rich. For, according to Smith, it led the rich 'to make nearly the same distribution of the necessaries of life, which would have been made, had the earth been divided into equal portions among all its inhabitants'.[51] For Smith, in other words, the progress of 'natural liberty' stood in place of a politics of redistribution.

∽

To cite these contrasts is only another way of making the obvious point that what changed the perspective of radicalism between the 1760s and the 1790s were the American and French Revolutions: particularly the revolt of the American colonies, the declaration of the American Republic and the defeat of the British by the Americans and the French, in all of which Paine played a prominent part. Of special importance was the effect of the American Revolution upon radical opinion in the decade before the French Revolution. For the impact made by this momentous sequence of events upon radical thinking in France was quite different from that in Britain. In fact, the American Revolution opened up a fundamental divergence between the horizons of radicals in the two countries, which was to have a lasting effect. It also helps to explain why British radicalism, despite its Gallic sympathies, found it difficult to fathom the direction of French thinking once the Revolution had begun.

In Britain, the effect of the loss of the American colonies was to reinforce the already widespread assumption, shared by radicals and Whigs alike, that since the accession of George III in 1760 the balance of the constitution had been upset. The constitution had been undermined by the secret ambitions of the executive through its sinister employment of patronage and corruption. Regeneration, narrowly interpreted by the Whigs, meant 'economical reform' – the reduction of posts and sinecures at the government's disposal. Among radicals, it meant more frequent parliaments and a broader or more representative electorate. It could even mean manhood suffrage. 'No taxation without representation' had been the slogan of the colonists; and it was not difficult to extend this principle to Britain, where each paid taxes and each possessed in his (or very rarely her) labour a property, so it was claimed, with as much right to be represented as any other form of property.

But although the American crisis inspired novel demands among a minority of radicals, the majority, especially after the end of the war in 1783, were on the defensive. Radicals were demoralised by the Fox–North coalition, widely regarded as a shameful display of political opportunism and they showed little appetite for fundamental change. Thus, despite Whig and radical agitation against George III's abuse of the constitution, no one proposed that Britain should follow the American example and become a republic. Richard Price in 1787 rejected the accusation of republicanism in this sense as 'a very groundless suspicion' and added,

'What I here say of myself I believe to be true of the whole body of British subjects among Protestant Dissenters.' He regarded 'our mixed form of government' as 'better adapted than any other to this country, and in theory excellent'. [52] In a mixed form of government, each element – King, Lords and Commons – fulfilled its legitimate function. The call for the 'purification', or 'restoration', of this constitution was socially cautious. It was in tune with a political climate in which calls for moral reform were far more widespread than political demands. In Britain, the 1780s was marked by Whig and radical division, by the revival of a new form of Toryism led by Pitt and by the growing strength of evangelicalism in the church.

Among French reformers, by contrast, respect for the English mixed form of government diminished. Admiration for the English constitution and English letters had been widespread during the time of Montesquieu and Voltaire, but the effect of the American Revolution and British defeat was to bring to the fore currents of thought never impressed by the English model of constitutional freedom. The writings of the Physiocrats in the 1760s provided one powerful source of criticism of mixed government. However contentious their proposal of a legal despot standing above the contending interests and imposing laws of 'natural order', many agreed with their assumption that only a unified source of power could withstand the entrenched interests of the aristocracy. There was also growing agreement with their belief that the dilution of power entailed in mixed government, with its attendant evils of privilege, corruption and disorder, was pushing Britain into decline.[53] The decline in the prestige of mixed government also reinforced an egalitarian and anti-aristocratic strand of criticism in France. The entrenched assumption common to so many forms of early modern republicanism of the need for a virtuous aristocracy gave way to a more radical questioning of the aristocracy's political and economic *raison d'être*. Writing in 1786, Condorcet observed that 'the spectacle of the equality that reigns in the United States and which assures its peace and prosperity, can also be useful to Europe. We no longer believe here, in truth, that nature has divided the human race into three or four orders, like the class of solipeds, and that one of these orders is also condemned to work much and eat little.'[54]

Finally, the success of the Americans led to a renewal and modernisation of republican thought. By the late 1780s, the idea that republics were largely confined to the ancient world and were suitable only in small homogeneous city states – still unchallenged in Britain – was no longer universally accepted in France. In particular, the Société Gallo-Américaine argued that the republicanism of the United States should be adopted in Europe, while from 1787 the inner core of the future Girondins – the group gathered around Brissot and Clavière – blamed the aristocracy for the crisis of the French state and called for the creation of a modern commercial republic freed from the hierarchy of rank.

Paine visited Paris several times in the 1780s and, through

Benjamin Franklin and the Société des Amis des Noirs, was acquainted with both Condorcet and Morellet and the group around Brissot. This together with his American experience also explains why Paine's radicalism was so different from that of his British contemporaries.[55] As Richard Whatmore has recently demonstrated, the difficulty of situating Paine's thought largely disappears once it is seen that his principal sources of inspiration were American and French, rather than English.[56] Paine had criticised mixed government as far back as *Common Sense* in 1776.

Almost alone among British radicals in the 1780s and 1790s, Paine was openly contemptuous of the supposed virtues of the English mixed constitution. 'In mixed governments there is no responsibility: the parts cover each other till responsibility is lost; and the corruption that moves the machine, contrives at the same time its own escape.' English government was without popular origins; it had begun with the conquest and remained a 'despotism' which the vaunted liberties of Parliament had done little to mitigate. Subjects were left with nothing more than the right of petitioning, but so far as Parliament itself was concerned, 'though the parts may embarrass each other, the whole has no bounds'.[57]

Secondly, and again in line with the French, Paine was openly hostile to the aristocracy. In Paine's opinion, what was required in Britain was not the restoration of a 'balanced constitution', but 'a revolution in the system of government'. 'Conquest and tyranny, at some earlier period, dispossessed man of his rights, and he is now recovering them.' The aristocracy arose out of governments founded on conquest. They 'are not the farmers who work the land, and raise the produce, but are the mere consumers of the rent; and when compared with the active world are the drones, a seraglio of males, who neither collect the honey nor form the hive, but exist only for lazy enjoyment'.[58]

But in at least one crucial respect Paine remained closer to his American experience than to the working assumptions of his French allies. This concerned the meaning of the word republic. For as far back as *Common Sense*, to Paine this meant a society without a monarchy or hereditary succession. 'Monarchy and succession have laid (not this or that kingdom only) but the world in blood and ashes.'[59] In France, at least until 1791, there was little support for a republic in this sense. In the 1780s, Condorcet had thought of himself as a republican in the same sense as his mentor, Turgot. Being a republican meant governing in the interests of the public good, which was quite possible under the aegis of an enlightened monarch. For, as he stated in his observations on the American Revolution in 1786, 'in terms of public happiness, a republic with tyrannical laws can fall far short of a monarchy'.[60]

In this and in other respects, the American model was not thought by most radicals to be transferable to Europe. First, it was argued, America was not really a large modern state comparable to European monarchies, but a federation of small republics. Secondly, its population – slaves aside – lived in conditions of relative equality and ease without the burden of a hereditary aristocracy and a feudal past. Finally, limitless access to land and agricultural self-sufficiency meant that America was not cursed with the extremes of wealth and poverty found in European commercial societies.

Up until the early years of the Revolution these remained basic but largely academic points of difference between Paine and his French friends. Whatever the ultimate destiny of the French nation, few before the summer of 1791 wished to question the credentials of the new 'King of the French'. But on 21 June 1791, the unanticipated happened. Louis fled Paris with his family, leaving a note reneging upon everything to which he had formally assented since the fall of the Bastille. Two days later, on 23 June, he was captured at Varennes and brought back to Paris. Now the question of the monarchy became an immediate practical issue. Faced with the double dealing of the king, Paine's closest associates, Condorcet, Brissot, Clavière and others, came round to his position. They founded a journal, *Le Républicain*, which argued that national unity necessitated a republic and Louis's expulsion.

The position adopted by Paine, Condorcet and others was challenged by the Abbé Sieyès in an article published in *Le Moniteur* on 6 July 1791. For Sieyès, who followed Hobbes on the question of sovereignty, the essential question was: who possesses the final power of decision-making. A monarch was better suited than a senate, weighed down 'under a multitude of Reports of Committees', to make 'the

individual decision'. The choice to be made was not therefore between republic and monarchy, but between what he
called monarchy and 'polyarchy'. Was the executive to be
appointed by a monarch or a national assembly? Ought the
apex of the state be considered as a 'platform' or as a 'point'?
'Polyarchy', Sieyès feared, was likely to lead to the formation of a new irresponsible senatorial aristocracy or of an
elective mode 'sometimes accompanied with a civil war'.[61]

These questions, rather than the objections of Burke,
set the agenda of *Rights of Man: Part Two*, which Paine
composed in the autumn and winter of 1791–2. This was
what also accounted for both Paine's radical reshaping of
Smith's account of commercial society and his dramatic
proposals to end poverty through a programme of social
insurance and redistributory taxation. One chapter was
explicitly addressed to Sieyès, but its title – 'Of the Old and
New Systems of Government' – really defined the book as
a whole. Paine's aim was to build his case for a republic
without a monarch upon the example of America, 'the only
real republic in character and in practice'. But in order to
make that case, he had to demonstrate how American conditions could be made applicable to Europe, and in the first
instance England.[62]

Sieyès had assumed that without a single and coherent
locus of decision-making, order might break down into
chaos. Paine in response argued that a 'great part of that
order which reigns among mankind is not the effect of government', and that 'the mutual dependence and reciprocal

interest which man has upon man, and all parts of the community upon each other, create the great chain of connection which holds it together'. In order to minimise the importance of Sieyès' objection, Paine made use of a radically simplified reading of Smith. The 'unnatural and retrograde order' which Smith blamed for the bellicose interstate politics of mercantilism, Paine simply equated with the rule of the aristocracy and the legacy of conquest. On the other hand, Smith's 'natural progress of opulence', which had wondrously continued 'beneath the long accumulating load of discouragement and oppression', only awaited the removal of 'government on the old system'. 'Old' government supported itself 'by keeping up a system of war'; the 'New System of Government' was not the product of conquest, but 'a delegation of power for the common benefit of society'.[63]

It was 'the old system of government' which was responsible for the 'hordes of miserable poor with which old countries abound'. The poverty of the poor was mainly the result of the taxation exacted by 'the old system of government' for the purpose of waging war. Smith in *The Wealth of Nations* argued that the advantages of living in modern civilised societies could easily be observed by comparing the situation of 'an industrious and frugal peasant' in Europe with that of 'many an African king, the absolute master of the lives and liberties of ten thousand native savages'. But, according to Paine, under existing conditions this was not true: '[A] great portion of mankind, in what are called civilised countries, are in a state of poverty and wretchedness, far below the condition of an Indian.'[64] Only when the old system of government had disappeared could the full potential of 'civilisation' be realised.

Like Condorcet, Paine strongly associated progress with universal education and the transition from superstition to reason. Monarchy could not be part of the new order according to Paine, because the monarchy, the aristocracy and the hereditary principle were associated with ignorance. 'Kings succeed each other, not as rationals, but as animals. Can we then be surprised at the abject state of the human mind in monarchical countries when the government itself is formed on such an abject levelling system?' Perhaps, somewhat tongue in cheek, Paine inverted the conventional argument which associated the republic with small states and the ancient world, by arguing that the modern principle of representation, unknown to the ancients, was perfectly suited to a large commercial republic, or to what Sieyès would have called a 'polyarchic' form. For only this form could take proper account of the complexities of the modern division of labour 'which requires a knowledge … which can be had only from the various parts of society'. 'It is an assemblage of practical knowledge, which no individual can possess', and therefore as ill-adapted to monarchy as to ancient 'simple' democracy. This was principle of American 'representation ingrafted upon democracy'. 'What Athens was in miniature, America will be in magnitude.'[65]

Finally, and perhaps most importantly, the possibility of a republic like that of the United States depended upon a rough equality and moderate differences of wealth. In Europe, Sieyès' spectre of civil war and a new aristocracy could be prevented if measures were taken to remove the power of the aristocracy or prevent the emergence of a new aristocracy in its place. Together with aristocracies went the manipulation of a factional and ignorant poor. In England, Paine noted, primogeniture was 'one of the principal sources of corruption at elections'.[66] This was why both Condorcet and Paine attached as much importance to universal education and redistributive taxation as they did to the provision of social security. Together, intervention in these three areas would create the material and mental conditions in which a modern republic could flourish in Europe. The more conservative plan proposed by Sieyès would mean not only the retention of the monarchy, but also the continuation of a distinction between 'active' and 'passive' citizenship as a way of keeping the poor at bay.

But according to Paine, this was not the way to ensure the security and stability of the republic. Similar restrictions of the franchise after 1795, as Paine argued in *Agrarian Justice* in 1797, led to Babouvist and royalist plots. The plan he proposed to the Directory in *Agrarian Justice* was designed to consolidate support for the revolution and preserve the rich from depradation. The argument was similar in *Part Two* of the *Rights of Man*: the social measures were designed to ensure that 'the poor as well as the rich, will then be interested in the support of government, and the cause and apprehension of riots and tumults will cease'.[67] His thinking in this area had no doubt been helped, not only by the general proposals of Condorcet, but also by the particular deliberations of the Comité de Mendicité under the chairmanship of the duc de La Rochefoucauld, in which relief was treated as an aspect of citizenship. A summary of their proceedings compiled in 1792 by Bernard d'Airy declared that 'every man has a right to subsistence through work, if he is able-bodied; and to free assistance if he is unable to work'. Assistance was no longer to be regarded as a 'favour', but as a 'duty' and a 'national responsibility'.[68] In France, given the hostility of much of the clergy to the new régime, it had been seen as a matter of political urgency to secure the loyalty of the poor to the new order by removing welfare from the control of the church.

ᑐ

This, then, was the reasoning which lay behind what the British critics perceived as the most threatening and subversive message of the French Revolution. Without a corrupt and powerful aristocracy to bribe the poor and without a priesthood to inhibit their powers to reason, but with an educated citizenry able to both adjust to the changing pattern of the economy and take seriously its civic responsibilities, a new era would begin. As Paine read Smith, the growth of commerce had brought 'the old system of government to its present crisis: if commerce were permitted to act to the universal extent it is capable, it would extirpate the system of war and produce a revolution in the uncivilised state of governments'. 'The present age will hereafter merit to be called "the Age of Reason", and the present generation will appear to the future as the Adam of a new world.'[69]

The first attempt to plan a world without poverty took shape, not as a response to problems of industry, but as part of an ambition to transplant the conditions of success of the young American republic to European soil. Although it was presented as a plan to overhaul the English tax system and abolish the Poor Rate, it was elaborated as part of a debate in France about what should happen after the king had gone back on his acceptance of the Revolution.[70] What was intended was not a welfare state, but the assembling of political conditions in which an informed citizenry could govern itself according to reason.

The proposals put forward by Condorcet and Paine built upon two major intellectual and institutional advances of the second half of the eighteenth century, together with a major shift in the radical stance towards the aristocracy. It was a programme which employed 'the calculus of prob-abilities' to make possible a programme which dispensed with the Poor Law and broke down the traditional notion of poverty into a number of predictable problems to be expected in the lifecycle of the average citizen. It made use of Smith's focus on investment rather than consumption as the crucial feature in the development of commercial socie-ties to suggest how individuals could exert greater control over the course of their lives. It also enabled a sharpening of some of the anti-aristocratic implications of Smith's argument, in particular an implicit distinction between this system of war and 'the civil state', that is, the operation of the parish and the judicial system – all areas which Hegel would characterise as belonging to the sphere of 'the police' in civil society rather than to the political state as such.

Finally, the proposals of Condorcet and Paine appeared as the culmination of a growing trend from the 1740s to incorporate the poor within civil society, perhaps as a result of four decades of economic growth and relative prosperity. This meant treating them as entitled to education, high wages and 'the decencies' of life. The emphasis was upon the commonality of mankind – the narrow differences which Smith discerned between the prince and the street porter – on the humanity of the poor and their capacity to participate in the culture of their more fortunate contemporaries. To consider them as fellow citizens, as they were commonly being considered in revolutionary countries, was no more than a logical next step in the process. But from the mid-1790s this trend was brought to an abrupt halt as British public opinion was made aware of the true extent of the political, social and religious radicalism of the French Revolution.

11

THE REACTION
IN BRITAIN

The effigy of Thomas Paine was, with great solemnity, drawn on a sledge from Lincoln Castle to the gallows, and then hanged, amidst a vast multitude of spectators. After being suspended the usual time it was taken to the Castle-hill and there hung on a gibbet post erected for that purpose. In the evening a large fire was made under the effigy, which … was consumed to ashes, amidst the acclamations of many hundreds of people, accompanied with a grand band of music playing 'God Save the King'.

It has been estimated that in the winter of 1792–3, effigies of Paine were burnt in 300 or so towns and villages in England and Wales. The intensity of the reaction was an indication of the magnitude of the felt threat. His *Rights of Man* was one of the bestsellers of the century; 250,000 copies had been sold by 1793. A London merchant wrote to Henry Dundas, the Home Secretary:

Payne is a dangerous book for any person who does not share in the spoil to be left alone with and it appears that the book is now made as much a standard book in this country, as Robinson Crusoe & the Pilgrims Progress, & that if it has not its effect today, it will tomorrow.[2]

The Evangelical and abolitionist leader William Wilberforce was equally anxious. William Hey of Leeds had informed him that 'immense pains are now taken to make the lower class of the people discontented, and to excite rebellion. Paine's mischievous work on "the Rights of Man" is compressed into a sixpenny pamphlet, and is sold and given away in profusion.' Wilberforce replied to Hey that he did not fear 'a speedy commotion', since 'almost every man of property in the kingdom' was 'a friend of civil order' and 'if a few mad-headed professors of liberty and equality were to attempt to bring their theories into practice, they would be crushed in an instant'. But he still feared 'a gathering storm' ahead. He was anxious that the country might provoke the 'judgements of an incensed God'. For what incurred his 'deepest gloom' was 'the prevailing profligacy of the times, and above all, that self-sufficiency, and proud and ungrateful forgetfulness of God, which is so general in the higher ranks of life'. He was therefore thinking of 'proposing to the Archbishop of Canterbury to suggest the appointment of a day of fasting and humiliation'.[3]

Alarm about the French Revolution had first been sounded by Burke. His *Reflections on the Revolution in*

France of 1790 began life as a response to Richard Price's 'Discourse on the Love of Our Country' delivered at the meeting house in the Old Jewry on 4 November 1789. The purpose of Price's 'Discourse' was to commemorate the revolution of 1688 and to welcome the beginnings of the revolution in France. Although Price spoke of 'the right to chuse our own governors, to cashier them for misconduct, and to frame government for ourselves' as one of the achievements of the 1689 Revolution Settlement, he did not move beyond existing radical demands for a balanced constitution within a framework of 'mixed government'. In practice, this meant a programme of parliamentary reform and a reiteration of the Dissenters' campaign for the repeal of the Test and Corporation Act. Price's assumption was that France would follow the pattern set in 1688 and democratically enlarged in the American Revolution of 1776. He concluded his address, '[A]fter sharing in the benefits of one Revolution, I have been spared to be a witness to two other Revolutions, both glorious'; and he reiterated the *nunc dimittis* – the words of the aged priest Simeon on the occasion of the first presentation of Christ in the Temple – 'Lord, lettest thou thy servant depart in peace, for mine eyes have seen thy salvation.'[4]

Burke fiercely contested the assumption that 1688 gave the people the right to 'cashier' their governors. In a calculated move to jolt Price's address away from the consensual terms of constitutionalist rhetoric, he compared Price's use of the *nunc dimittis* with that of the Reverend Hugh Peters at the trial of Charles I in 1648. Price's 'sally' differed 'only in place and time, but agrees perfectly with the spirit and letter of the rapture of 1648'.[5] In a powerful invocation of the silent majority, he also sowed suspicion about the Dissenters and other French sympathisers as true representatives of British opinion.

> Because half a dozen grasshoppers under a fern make the field ring with their importunate chink, whilst thousands of great cattle reposed beneath the shadow of the British oak, chew the cud and are silent, pray do not imagine that those who make the noise are the only inhabitants of the field.

Burke was deeply sceptical of the capacity of a government based upon 'the rights of man' to create happiness. Human distress was largely the result of individual moral failure, not of the imperfection of institutions. Nor did the leaders of this revolution inspire confidence. Unlike 1688, the Revolution in France was led by persons without legislative experience, disgruntled lawyers and malcontent 'men of quality'. In place of the ancient nobility – 'the Corinthian capital of polished society' – and in place of a church which preached obedience to the sovereign power, this Revolution was sweeping away deference to social rank, only to usher in a tyrannical democratic majority and establish a new nobility of money-lenders and stock speculators. Finally, and most seriously, without any real awareness of the consequences of their actions, the revolutionaries thought their confiscations of the lands and possessions of the church had put into question all established rights of property in France.

When Burke's *Reflections* first appeared, most thought its stance farfetched. Even as the Revolution became more extreme, few were prepared to share Burke's lament for the passing of 'the age of chivalry' or his defence of the *ancien régime*. But his attack on Price and his friends as a potential Jacobin fifth column was picked up in the provincial press where it helped to re-ignite Tory and Anglican hostility towards the pretensions of the Dissenters, resulting in some places in crowd actions, most notoriously in Birmingham, where the house of Joseph Priestley was destroyed on Bastille Day 1791.

Burke's approach was partially vindicated by the publication of the two parts of Paine's *Rights of Man* in 1791 and 1792. Here was proof that the aim of French revolutionaries was not to create a new form of 'mixed government', but to establish an egalitarian republic. Moderate reformers hastened to distance themselves from Paine's programme. The veteran campaigner for political reform Christopher Wyvill, in his *Defence of Dr Price*, deplored 'the mischievous effects' of Paine's approach in exciting 'the lowest classes of the People to acts of violence and injustice' and was especially incensed by the social proposals contained in the second part of the *Rights of Man*. In April 1792 he therefore proposed that the London Constitutional Society dissociate itself from a programme which held out to the poor 'annuities to be had out of the superfluous wealth of the Rich'.[6]

The reservations of moderates did little to stem the phe-
nomenal spread of Painite ideas in 1792. Well-supported
democratic associations were established in twenty major
towns, with 'divisions' or 'tythings' formed in the surrounding countrysides. In the summer of 1792 the government decided to prosecute the *Rights of Man* in response
and issued a proclamation against seditious writing. In
December of that year, it even set forth a royal proclamation summoning the militia to counter 'the radical invasion'.
Governmental action was in turn massively reinforced by
the initiative of John Reeves in forming loyalist associations
to counteract sedition. After a few months 1,500 associations had been formed.

Such was the background to the Paine burnings of
1792–3. They were often organised by loyalist associations,
both to demonstrate the extent of their local support and
to intimidate radicals in surrounding areas. Loyalists also
put pressure on town officials and local employers to dis-
criminate against the employment of radicals, compelled
publicans to deny radicals the hire of public rooms and
prosecuted prominent activists. By 1794, Britain was at war
with France and events in France were taking an ever more
bloodthirsty turn. Loyalist propaganda dwelt more and
more insistently upon 'the bloody *bonnet rouge*, the piked
head, and the guillotine'. They had been able to assemble a
mass movement which, though uneven on the ground, was
able to push radicals into retreat.[7]

In London, Norwich and Sheffield, radicals still dared to

defy the increasingly repressive climate. In 1795, two leading members of the London Corresponding Society, Thomas Hardy and Horne Took, were acquitted of treason by a London jury, and the king was jeered by crowds as he proceeded through Hyde Park. But 1795 was a turning point. After the Treasonable Practices and Seditious Meetings Acts ('the Gagging Acts'), open defiance ceased. Activists found it increasingly difficult to act or assemble, even in radical strongholds, without suffering legal or financial persecution.

Loyalist pressure was not simply a matter of control over the streets, it also narrowed the scope of intellectual debate and misrepresented its contents. The situation was worst in Scotland, where in a notorious series of sedition trials of 1793–4, radicals were transported for sentences of seven to fourteen years simply for 'exciting disaffection to government'. Political hysteria also reached the academy. Dugald Stewart, Adam Smith's best-known disciple and first biographer, delivered his 'Account of the Life and Writings of Adam Smith' to the Royal Society of Edinburgh in 1793.[8] On the evidence of *The Wealth of Nations*, Smith was an unqualified supporter of high wages, far more tolerant of combinations of labourers than of masters. Indeed, Malthus chided him for confusing 'the happiness of nations' with 'the happiness and comfort of the lower orders of society which is the most numerous class in every nation'.[9] He was not a critic of the Poor Laws except of the vexations caused to the poor by removals under the Law of Settlement, nor is there any record of his opposing whatever relief measures might be necessary in cases of famine or high prices, since the problem simply did not arise. He was not in favour of primogeniture, and nor did he favour an established church.

In the fiercely counter-revolutionary atmosphere of Scotland at the time, it is perhaps not surprising that Stewart should have minimised the importance of Smith's political preferences. In so doing, however, he initiated a distinction between political economy and politics which was to have long-lasting effects, while his politically bloodless re-reading of Smith provided one of the sources of political economy's reputation among radicals and romantics as 'the dismal science' with 'a heart of flint'. Stewart admitted that Smith's 'speculations', along with those of 'Quesnai, Turgot, Compomanes, Beccaria and others, have aimed at the improvement of society'. But, he hastened to reassure his audience, 'such speculations' … have no tendency to unhinge established institutions, or to inflame the passions of the multitude. The improvements they recommend are to be effected by means too gradual and slow in their operation, to warm the imaginations of any but of the speculative few; and in proportion as they are adopted, they consolidate the political fabric, and enlarge the basis upon which it rests.'[10] Stewart even obscured the undeniable fact that Smith identified with the religious scepticism of Hume, let alone the yet more uncomfortable fact that Smith's *Theory of Moral Sentiments* was at that time much studied by the Philosophe party among the French Revolutionaries as offering a non-Christian moral theory.[11]

But worse was to come, and in 1794 he himself was obliged to disown his former acquaintance with the Philosophe party. Two Scottish law lords asked him to retract a small reference to Condorcet in his *Philosophy of the Human Mind* and to renounce 'in an open and manly manner … every word you had ever uttered in favour of doctrines which had led to so giant a mischief'. From 1 February 1793, Britain was at war with France, a war originally advocated primarily by the Girondin party. Perhaps it was the association of Condorcet with the Girondins which had led Stewart temporarily to concur with Burke's judgement on the fall of Brissot in the summer of 1793:

> His faction having obtained their stupendous and unnatural power, by rooting out of the minds of his unhappy countrymen every principle of religion, morality, loyalty, fidelity and honour, discovered, that when authority came into their hands, it would be a matter of no small difficulty for them to carry on government on the principles by which they had destroyed it.[12]

Stewart complied with the request and accordingly expressed regret for 'mentioning with respect the name of Condorcet'.[13]

The discussion of Paine's ideas was scarcely less febrile. Despite the widespread anxiety expressed by magistrates about the appeal of Paine's ideas on taxation and social insurance, those proposals were barely discussed. Instead, as Greg Claeys has concluded from an examination of 600 contributions to the pamphlet debate on the Revolution, Paine was simply treated as a 'leveller', as an advocate of economic equality.[14]

This also meant that there was relatively little discussion of the one significantly redistributive element in Paine's programme: the proposal to employ progressive taxation to end the practice of primogeniture. Such a measure, Paine hoped, would lead to the break-up of great estates and the dismantling of the large concentrations of aristocratic power and wealth which had been assembled through feudal devices like primogeniture and entail. Paine's criticism of primogeniture was very similar to that of Smith, which had been made largely on the basis of utility.[15] A minority of more perceptive or scrupulous critics took account of Paine's specific aim but questioned the assumption that the egalitarian conditions of an agrarian yet non-feudal society like America's could be transplanted across the Atlantic. They did not think it possible to form a commercial republic in Europe more egalitarian than those of Venice or Holland.

The majority, however, insisted on interpreting Paine as if he were advocating the return of the ancient republic or the reversion to some primitive community of goods. They did so by treating his argument as if it were based solely upon an appeal to 'natural rights'. Critics referred overwhelmingly to the argument that Paine had put forward in

Part One of the *Rights of Man* – an argument which took natural rights back to the state of nature and Adam and Eve – in order to refute Burke's denial of the right of the people to move beyond the parliamentary settlement of 1688. Presenting this point as if it were the premise of an argument for economic equality, Loyalists argued that all rights were civil; that there had been no natural equality and no rights in the state of nature; that Adam had not been equal with his sons; and that the society described in Genesis was most likely to have been a monarchy. Social hierarchy was therefore a natural development and it was appropriate that sovereignty should reside not in the people, but in the legislature. All this was designed to underpin their main contention that the assumption of equality which informed Paine's vision of society was incompatible with the opulence which characterised a commercial society like that in Britain.

The particular accusations flung at Paine in this debate seem even stranger when set alongside English Poor Law practice at the time.[16] For while many of the critics of the French Revolution argued that inequality was inseparable from the benefits of commercial society and feared the consequences of leading the poor to imagine that they possessed a right to relief, the reality was that a right to relief was already firmly inscribed within the existing Poor Law system. This reality, legal as well as moral, was stated by a legal expert in 1793: '[T]he right to receive a compensation for their labour, adequate to their necessary wants, while they have a capability of labour is certainly due to them; and the right of maintenance from the more opulent classes of society when that capability to labour is passed, is another debt which owes them.' 'The occupation of the labourer,' he maintained, 'subjects him to acute illness, chronic disorders, and at length to old age, decrepitude, and impotence.' 'Without the aid of his more opulent neighbours, or what is infinitely to the credit of this nation, without the interference of the Godlike laws of his country, this useful class of our countrymen would sink in the arms of famine or despair.'[17]

Nor were these rights new. The practice of local tax-based relief had been in existence since the time of the Henrician reformation as a systematisation of parish charity. That process had resulted in 1572 in an act enabling justices of the peace to provide relief by means of a parochial tax, codified in 1597–8 and set out in permanent form in the Elizabethan Poor Law of 1601. Although it was not the main intention of the act, the right to relief was strongly reinforced by the Act of Settlement of 1662. For, although an applicant for relief who did not comply with statutory residence requirements could be removed from a particular parish, his or her removal could only be to another parish where they possessed such an entitlement. Therefore, vexatious though the operation of the Law of Settlement undoubtedly often was, it institutionalised the duty of relief within the parochial system.

Tax-based local relief had been practised in other parts of Europe in the sixteenth century, but only in England did it survive in an elaborated form through to the eighteenth century; and only in the period after 1750 did the singularity and extent of the English Poor Law become a matter of repeated comment.[18] One of the hardships created by the system, as noticed by continental observers, was the lack of any administrative mechanism to spread the very uneven burdens placed upon rich and poor parishes. François, the 18-year-old future duc de La Rochefoucauld-Liancourt, chair of the Comité de Mendicité in the early years of the French Revolution, remarked upon this inequality of local tax burden on a fact-finding visit to East Anglia in 1782. Recording his impressions of Yarmouth, he commented, 'The poor rate is alarming: 10 shillings in the pound. I have never managed to understand the explanation of so exorbitant a tax.'[19]

A more common complaint within England itself was not so much the distribution, but the *level* of the tax, which rose steadily from the 1760s. From then onwards, calls for its abolition became increasingly frequent. The poor rate, it was argued, was a tax upon the industrious to support the idle, and the case of industrious Scotland without a Poor Law was often cited to prove that such a law was unnecessary (though the counter-case of Ireland, also without a Poor Law, demonstrated that simple correlations were inconclusive). Interestingly, however, in the decade after the outbreak of the Revolution in 1789, rate-based expenditure increased even more rapidly than before.

In part, this was a response to years of exceptional and

visible hardship like 1795; in part, to the fear of revolution. Magistrates were empowered to set levels of relief outside the workhouse supplementing the inadequate wages of working men with families, particularly in years of scarcity. This resorting to a 'rate in aid of wages' – the so-called Speenhamland System – was to become a stock item in an endlessly repeated Victorian horror story about the bad old days before the New Poor Law. But it was mainly justified at the time on prudential grounds. Nor was it confined to extravagant local authorities. Central government also appeared keen to ensure generous scales of relief. In a proposed Poor Law Bill of 1796, Pitt referred approvingly to 'the labouring poor' and urged, 'Let us … make relief, in cases where there are a number of children, a matter of right, and an honour instead of a ground for opprobrium and contempt. This will make a large family a blessing and not a curse.'[20] Pitt opposed Whitbread's proposal for a minimum wage. But his own bill included a gamut of proposals for the alleviation of the condition of the poor – family allowances, a rate in aid of wages, money to purchase a cow, schools of industry for poor children, reclamation of waste land, a relaxation of the Law of Settlement and measures to assist the provision of insurance against sickness and old age.[21] It is clear that politicians and magistrates, whatever the pronouncements of their propagandists, had kept one eye on the suggestions emanating from the Comité de Mendicité in France.

The debate between Whitbread and Pitt was between two politicians, both of whom were attempting to devise measures in the spirit of Smith to alleviate the economic hardship of the 'labouring poor' in the mid-1790s. But even those followers of Smith who opposed such measures were against any drastic change in the practice of relief. Frederick Eden, in his *State of the Poor*, disliked the measures proposed by both Whitbread and Pitt. He thought that a right to employment or maintenance might deter industriousness. But it would be an even greater mistake to remove such 'rights'. The 'poor' or 'the labouring classes' were a new class created by freeing the people from bondage to the soil and through the rise of manufacture. Earlier there had been no 'poor', only 'slaves'. Freed from dependence upon feudal lords, however, they still expected help when incapacitated by sickness or old age. Like other legislation set in place in an earlier age to meet different circumstances, the Poor Laws should be reformed, not abolished.

Seen in this context, Paine's detailed proposals do not seem so outlandish. He was merely attempting to shift the emphasis from cure to prevention. As he himself put it, comparing his proposals in *Agrarian Justice* to the practice of the English Poor Laws:

> It is the practice of what has unjustly obtained the name of civilisation (and the practice merits not to be called either charity or policy) to make some provision for persons becoming poor and wretched only at the time they become so. Would it not, even as a matter of economy, be far better to adopt means to prevent their becoming poor? This can

best be done by making every person when arrived at the age of twenty-one years an inheritor of something to begin with.[22]

But by 1797, the year in which Paine made this proposal, the climate of opinion had begun to change fundamentally and in such a way that, within a few years, the mid-90s poverty proposals of Paine and Pitt alike had been consigned to oblivion.

Whether radicalism collapsed or went underground, as Edward Thompson argued in *The Making of the English Working Class*, is still a matter of historical debate. But of the magnitude of the shift in public opinion there can be no doubt. Disenchantment with the failures and shock at the sanguinary excesses of the Revolution were compounded by a more general welling-up of wartime patriotic sentiment. Never more so than in the years 1797 and 1798, when it was fanned by mutinies in the fleet, scares about French invasion and rebellion in Ireland. The impact of these events was manifest in the falling-out of former political allies, in political re-alignments, in a far greater intolerance of atheism and free thought, in a great intensification of the new evangelical religious culture which had been growing since the 1780s, and finally in what R. H. Tawney in a different context once described as 'a new medicine for poverty'.

Although religious themes were never absent from the debate about the Revolution, in the first half of the 1790s they remained subordinate. Burke, in *Reflections*, was excep-

tional in warning of 'the spirit of atheistical fanaticism …
in all the streets and places of public resort in Paris' and in
arguing that the new ecclesiastical establishment in France
was intended only to be 'temporary', and 'preparatory to
the utter abolition, under any of its forms, of the Christian
religion'.[23] The loyalist response to Paine largely focussed
upon a defence of the existing constitution and upon the
primitivist implications of his conception of rights. Pitt's
old Cambridge tutor, George Pretyman-Tomline, now a
bishop, in his *Charge Delivered to the Clergy of the Diocese
of Lincoln* of 1794, spent nine pages outlining the necessity
of the Christian principles of subordination and restraint
to the functioning of society, but only six lines on the religious basis of political obligation.[24] At the end of the *Rights
of Man* Paine congratulated himself that in the whole work,
'there is only a single paragraph upon religion'. But, as it
happened, that paragraph did touch the core of what was at
issue between the supporters and opponents of revolution.
His argument was that 'every religion is good that teaches
man to be good'.[25] The case for the perfectibility of man, and
hence for the elimination of poverty, stood or fell on the
question of whether human nature was inherently imperfect ('original sin') and therefore whether restraints needed
to be placed upon man's activity. The need to clear away
such impediments to the possibility of perfectibility was
strongly argued by Mary Wollstonecraft in 1794:

We must get entirely clear of all the notions drawn from

the wild traditions of original sin: the eating of the apple, the theft of Prometheus, the opening of Pandora's box and other tales too tedious to enumerate, on which priests have erected their tremendous structures of imposition, to persuade us, that we are naturally inclined to evil. [26]

But as revolutionary hopes gave way to disenchantment and the war acquired the dimensions of a struggle for national survival, the Christian element in the attack on notions of perfectibility became increasingly pronounced; sin and the vanity of human illusions about perfection were themes that the opponents of the Revolution were happy to throw back at its supporters. In one of the tracts of the leading Evangelical activist Hannah More, *The History of Mr Fantom, the New-fashioned Philosopher*, in answer to Mr Fantom, who has 'a plan … for relieving the miseries of the whole world', Mr Trueman objects:

But, sir, among all your abolitions, you must abolish human corruption before you can make the world quite as perfect as you pretend. You philosophers seem to me to be ignorant of the very first seed and principle of misery – sin, sir, sin. Your system of reform is radically defective; for it does not comprehend that sinful nature from which all misery proceeds. You accuse government of defects which belong to man, and, of course, to man collectively. Among your reforms you must reform the human heart.[27]

For supporters of the Revolution, like Mary Woll-stonecraft, the only excuse for the ferocity of the Parisians was that, under the monarchy, they had lost all confidence in the laws. As she stated in 1794, 'When justice, or the law is so partial, the day of retribution will come with the red sky of vengeance, to confound the innocent with the guilty. The mob were barbarous beyond the tiger's cruelty: for how could they trust a court that had so often deceived them, or expect to see its agents punished?'[28] But for its opponents, the Revolution became an example of what happens when Christian restraint upon the passions is removed. The need to restrain the poor and to inculcate in them the religious duty of submission to providence had already become prominent in the work of Sarah Trimmer, Hugh Berinton and others in the 1780s as a response to the Gordon Riots and the growth of pauperism. On the division between wealth and poverty, God's ordinance was treated by Christians, whether radical or conservative, as beyond human questioning. According to the Gospel of St Matthew, as Christ sat in the house of Simon the Leper, a woman came and poured a precious ointment over his head. The disciples strongly objected to 'this waste'. But Christ responded, 'Why trouble ye the woman for she hath wrought a good work upon me? For ye have the poor always with you; but me ye have not always.'

However unfortunate, the presence of the poor was inescapable. They formed a constituent part of the Christian cosmos.[29] For the good Christian, poverty was not a condition to be remedied, but the spur to the exercise of humility, the practice of charity and the striving for grace. John Wesley, when contemplating the horrors of poverty, found comfort in the promise of the Resurrection. Richard Price also considered that this life was only to be judged within the framework of the eternal. However full of temptations and tribulations the earthly journey, what mattered was the heavenly destination. In this sense, the path of the simple poor man might be easier and more straightforward than that of the pampered rich. But the argument was pressed with even greater insistence in the face of the revolutionary threat. According to William Wilberforce's *Practical View* of 1797:

In whatever class or order of society Christianity prevails, she sets herself to rectify the particular faults, or, if we would speak more distinctly, to counteract the particular mode of selfishness, to which that class is liable … Thus, softening the glare of wealth, and moderating the insolence of power, she renders the inequalities of the social state less galling to the lower orders, whom also she instructs, in their turn, to be diligent, humble, patient: reminding them that their more lowly path has been allotted to them by the hand of God; that it is their part faithfully to discharge its duties, and contentedly to bear its inconveniences; that the present state of things is very short; that the objects about which worldly men conflict so eagerly, are not worth the contest; that the peace of mind which Religion offers to all ranks indiscriminately, affords more true satisfaction than all the expensive pleasures which are beyond the poor man's reach.[30]

Christianity exposed the false promise of perfectibility. As Hannah More admonished 'women of rank and fortune' in 1799: '[T]he Gospel *can* make no part of a system in which the absurd idea of perfectibility is considered applicable to fallen creatures; in which the chimerical project of consummate earthly happiness (founded on the mad pretence of loving the poor better than God loves them) would defeat the divine plan, which meant this world for a scene of discipline, not of remuneration.'[31]

The strength of Christianity in the eyes of its defenders was not merely that it reconciled the poor to their subordination, but that through its conceptions of sin and redemption, punishment and atonement, it enforced morality in all classes of society and thus held society together, especially a commercial society in which self-interest was so much to the fore. According to Wilberforce again,

> Christianity in every way sets herself in direct hostility to selfishness, the mortal distemper of political communities. It might indeed be almost stated as the main object and chief concern of Christianity, to root out our natural selfishness, and to rectify the false standard which it imposes on us; with views, however, far higher than any which concern merely our temporal and social well-being.[32]

The point was also made polemically by Hannah More. The irreligious appeared to believe that a simulacrum of morality was as good as the thing itself. Hadn't that been the teaching of Mandeville? The half-understood implications of this 'philosopher's' idea were dramatised in the behaviour of William, Mr Fantom's manservant. Reprimanded by his master for serving guests at table while drunk, he replied 'very pertly', 'Sir, if I do get drunk now and then, I only do it for the good of my country, and in obedience to your wishes.' After being scolded 'in words not fit to be repeated', William again retorted: 'Why, sir, you are a philosopher … and I have often overheard you say to your company, that private vices are public benefits; and so I thought that getting drunk was as pleasant a way of doing good to the public as any, especially when I could oblige my master at the same time.'[33]

In the course of the 1790s, the Christian riposte to the Revolution and its English supporters also acquired an increasingly aggressive edge. If religion held society together, the irreligious were no longer an unfortunate but harmless minority, they became those who aimed at society's dissolution. Once again, Burke was one of the earliest and most consistent exponents of this view. Already in *Reflections* he referred to a 'literary cabal' which had 'formed something like a regular plan for the destruction of the Christian religion', and drew attention to a supposed conspiracy of the Bavarian *illuminati* (illuminist freemasons). Thereafter, he became ever more convinced that the events in France were a 'revolution of doctrine and theoretick dogma' designed to 'get rid of the clergy, and indeed of any form of religion', and that 'a system of French conspiracy' was 'gaining ground in every country'. 'Atheists', he remarked in 1791, were no longer like 'the old Epicureans, rather an unenterprising race'. Lately they had grown 'active, designing, turbulent and seditious', the 'sworn enemies to kings, nobility and priesthood. We have seen all the academicians at Paris, with Condorcet, the friend and correspondent of Priestley, at their head, the most furious of the extravagant republicans.'

He elaborated his interpretation most fully in 1796 in 'His Letters on a Regicide Peace'. Britain was at war with 'an armed doctrine' built upon regicide, Jacobinism and atheism. The origins of this revolution had been brought about by two sorts of men: the philosophers and the politicians. 'The philosophers had one predominant object, which they pursued with a fanatical fury, that is, the utter extirpation of religion.' Between them, the philosophers and the politicians had been responsible for 'a silent revolution in the moral world' which 'preceded the political and prepared it'.[34]

In the early 1790s, few followed Burke in believing that the Revolution had been the result of a philosophical plot to destroy Christianity. James Mackintosh, the leading Whig intellectual, protested in 1791 that 'the supposition of their conspiracy for the abolition of Christianity, is one of the most extravagant chimeras that ever entered the human imagination'. He argued that 'it was not against religion, but

against the Church that their *political* hostility was directed';
'their purpose was accomplished when the Priesthood was
disarmed'.[35] Attitudes changed dramatically in 1797 with the
publication of alleged proofs by the Abbé Barruel in France
and by John Robison in England that either the *philosophes* or
the freemasons and *illuminati*, or some combination of the
two, had brought about the Revolution and engineered the
fall of the monarchy. During the sitting of the Assembly of
Notables in 1788, according to Robison, the German *illuminati* with the assistance of allies like Mirabeau and Philippe
duc d'Orléans, sent a delegation to France. Their aim was to
abolish the laws which protected property, establish universal liberty and equality, 'and as necessary preparations for
all this, they intended to root out all religion and ordinary
morality … *This was all that the Illuminati could teach*, and
THIS WAS PRECISELY WHAT FRANCE HAS DONE.'[36]
According to popular versions of these arguments, the philosophers believed that religion had first to be overthrown
before it was possible to bring down the monarchy. The fact
of the publication of Paine's *Age of Reason* in 1796, an attack
on the morality, textual consistency and historical veracity
of the Bible, seemed to prove that irreligion, sedition and
support for the national enemy were closely linked. Paine's
declaration at the beginning of the book of his belief in God
and hope of an afterlife cut little ice.[37] Loyal and patriotic
support for 'mixed government' and for the existing hierarchy of ranks was now extended to encompass an allegiance
to the Church of England.

❦

Alongside the sharper attack upon the patriotism and good faith of the radicals in the later 1790s there developed a noticeably harsher stance towards the poor. Once again, Burke helped to set the trend. In the 'Letters on a Regicide Peace', he had already attacked 'the pulling jargon' of the 'labouring poor' as if their condition was in itself to be pitied, as opposed to those who through sickness, disability or old age were unable to work. This was 'trifling with the condition of mankind' and forgetting that it was 'the common doom of man that he must eat his bread by the sweat of his brow'.[38] In the posthumous publication of what might originally have been intended as a memorandum (evidently unheeded) to Pitt on how to deal with the near-famine food prices of 1795, Burke argued vehemently against government intervention. Labour was 'a commodity ... an article of trade'. 'It is not in breaking the laws of commerce, which are the laws of nature, and consequently the laws of God, that we are to place our hope of softening the Divine displeasure to remove any calamity under which we suffer, or which hangs over us.' 'To provide for us in our necessities is not in the power of government.' Burke railed against this 'political canting language'. 'Charity to the poor' was 'a direct and obligatory duty upon all Christians'. 'But let there be no lamentation of their condition ... Patience, labour, sobriety, frugality, and religion, should be recommended to them; all the rest is downright *fraud*.'[39] What was most remarkable about this document was that by the time

Burke's executors brought it out in a posthumous edition in 1800, his insistence upon absolute non-interference with market mechanisms, even in virtual famine conditions, was interpreted without quibble as an exposition of Smith's views on the topic.[40]

Exactly why Burke's view came to be assimilated so rapidly and unproblematically with that of Smith is unclear. But it was certainly in part the result of Malthus's *Essay on Population*, which had appeared in 1798. The full title of Malthus's work was *An Essay on the Principle of Population, as It Affects the Future Improvement of Society with Remarks on the Speculations of Mr Godwin, M. Condorcet and Other Writers*. This *Essay*, with its famous juxtaposition of population which 'when unchecked, increased in geometrical ratio' with 'subsistence for man' whose increase was only 'in an arithmetical ratio', was an exercise in natural theology. Not everyone considered that revolutionary visions of the end of poverty and inequality could simply be countered by the undigested mixture of Genesis and political economy found in the late Burke, or the unrelieved emphasis upon sin, atonement and the transitoriness of earthly life of the Evangelicals. For such readers, the *Essay* offered a more reasoned account of the impossibility of 'a society, all the members of which should live in ease, happiness and comparative leisure; and feel no anxiety about providing the means of subsistence for themselves and families'.[41]

Malthus came from a family well versed in enlightened speculation. His father had once entertained Rousseau and

Hume; and he himself had received part of his education at the famous Warrington Academy under the guidance of the prominent Unitarian and champion of 'rational dissent', Gilbert Wakefield. In 1784 he had entered Jesus College, Cambridge, which was at the time another renowned centre of theological liberalism. Although Malthus seems always to have been destined for the church, among his Cambridge friends were to be found those who were both radical and unorthodox, in particular his tutor, William Frend, to whom he remained close into later life. In 1787, Frend publicly renounced the Thirty-nine Articles of the Church of England and espoused Unitarianism; and in 1793, he was expelled from the university for political radicalism.[42] It is also indicative of the milieu within which Malthus moved that the *Essay* itself was published (anonymously) by the radical Joseph Johnson, who was also the publisher of Godwin and Wollstonecraft. The *Essay* was said to have been prompted by discussions between Malthus and his father about the utopian views set forth by William Godwin in his *Enquiry Concerning Political Justice* of 1793 and *Enquirer* of 1797. At the time, Malthus was a moderate Foxite Whig who opposed Pitt's coercion of British radicals and disliked Burke for his abandonment of the Foxite cause. Even after 1800, he remained a 'friend of peace' – one reason why he was attacked so vehemently by the Romantics, especially Coleridge and Southey. In later life, he continued to support the repeal of the Test and Corporation Acts, Catholic emancipation and moderate franchise reform of the kind put forward in 1832. [43]

The substantive content of Malthus's account was determined by its Christian form, that of a theodicy designed to explain the necessary presence of evil in a world created by an omnipotent, omniscient and benevolent God.[44] But there was nothing traditional about the theodicy Malthus constructed, and its impact spread far beyond the ranks of Christian believers. According once more to Dugald Stewart, principal intellectual heir to Smith and prominent Edinburgh Whig, the 'reasonings' of the *Essay*, 'in so far as they relate to the Utopian plans of Wallace, Condorcet and Godwin, are perfectly conclusive, and strike at the root of all such theories'.[45]

Until the end of the seventeenth century, theodicies were composed almost entirely out of the materials of revealed Christianity, especially Paul's reading of the Fall and Augustine's depiction of the hereditary transmission of sin to the posterity of Adam. Sin was a 'depravity' both of reason and of will conveyed through the act of generation, which was inherently sinful because mired in 'concupiscence'. That God saved some to receive the gift of 'final perseverance', and so be saved from eternal damnation, was entirely a matter of God's grace. Earthly life was a state of 'trial' and 'probation' spent in a perpetual striving to escape from the all-pervasive mesh of sin and corruption.

The hold of this grim doctrine, heavily underscored in Lutheran and Calvinist theologies and propagated uncompromisingly in the religious wars of the seventeenth century, loosened perceptibly after 1700. Confronted by a growing challenge from free thought, by enlightened notions of justice and by the beginnings of a historical and developmental approach to the Bible, the harsh edges of Augustinian and Calvinist doctrine yielded to a theology appealing as much to reason as to revelation. This was especially the case in eighteenth-century Britain, where the 1688 Settlement and a latitudinarian stance on questions of religious doctrine were designed to put to sleep the bloody conflicts of the previous century. Cambridge was the most important centre of this new liberal theology. It built upon Newton's vision of an orderly cosmos and evidence found in nature of the power, wisdom and goodness of God. Evil in the world was no more than the minimum necessary to accomplish God's purposes. It was from within this tradition of natural theology running from John Ray to Edmund Law and William Paley that Malthus composed his *Essay*.[46]

In *Political Justice*, William Godwin, himself a former dissenting minister, depicted the approach of a world in which evil, together with private property, government and punishment, would wither away. Godwin looked forward to a prospect described by Benjamin Franklin, in which mind would become omnipotent over matter and death itself might be abolished. According to Godwin, there was no original sin, nor any inherent differences between men. Man was an intellectually and morally progressive being; moral and political improvement ('perfectibility') followed from the increase of knowledge.

Pondering the depiction of 'luxury' by Mandeville and

its defence by Hume, Godwin conceded that without 'the spectacle of inequality', which provoked 'the persevering exertion' of the Barbarians, 'leisure which served the purpose of literature and art' would not have been possible. But, he went on, 'though inequality were necessary as the prelude to civilisation, it is not necessary to its support. We may throw down the scaffolding when the edifice is complete.' It was therefore only mistaken ideas of self-interest, not inherent drives or passions, which diverted man from 'benevolence'. As knowledge, and hence virtue, increased, man would become increasingly dependent upon reason alone. Both private property and marriage as forms of monopoly would be voluntarily relinquished and, since 'the pleasures of intel-lect' would be preferred to 'the pleasures of sense', sexual pleasure would eventually fade away.[47]

Malthus's natural theology aimed to refute Godwin, not by citing Scripture, but by 'turning our eyes to the book of Nature, where alone we can read God as he is'. One of Godwin's principal errors was to treat man as if he were a 'wholly intellectual' creature and could therefore be moved to give up private property through 'benevolence'. Malthus responded that it was to 'the established administration of property, and to the apparently narrow principle of self-love, that we are endebted … for everything … that distinguishes the civilised from the savage state'. It was not the unaided processes of mind which spurred men into action, but 'the wants of the body' that roused 'the brain of infant man into sentient activity'. If Godwin's commonwealth were brought into being and those 'stimulants to exertion, which arise from the wants of the body were removed from the mass of mankind, we have more reason to think they would be sunk to the level of brutes, from a deficiency of excitements, than that they would be raised to the ranks of philosophers by the possession of leisure'. No sufficient change had taken place in 'the nature of civilised man' to suggest that he might 'safely throw down the ladder' by which he had risen to his present 'eminence'.[48]

The progress of man from savagery to civilisation was not the product of the unaided and inherent activity of mind. The creation of mind was not the cause but the effect of a struggle of cosmic dimensions, in which 'the world, and this life' could be seen as 'a mighty process of God … for the creation and formation of mind; a process necessary, to awaken inert, chaotic matter into spirit'. And 'necessity' (the principle of population) provided the means by which man, 'as he really is, inert, sluggish, and averse from labour', was compelled into activity by God. 'The savage would slumber for ever under his tree unless he was roused from his torpor by the cravings of hunger, or the pinchings of cold.' Indeed, in this new and decidedly heterodox version of Christianity, original sin was no longer the product of *activity* – the disobedience of Adam and Eve in the Garden of Eden – but of *passivity*: 'The original sin of man, is the torpor and corruption of the chaotic matter, in which he may be said to be born.'[49]

This life was therefore no longer a state of 'trial' or 'probation' in which the Christian should accept his allotted rank with cheerfulness and humility; it was rather a state of 'universal exertion' whose strong and constantly operative … stimulus was 'the superiority of the power of population to the means of subsistence … Had population and food increased in the same ratio, it is probable that man might never have emerged from the savage state.' Inequality formed part of this divine scheme. 'If no man could hope to rise, or fear to fall, in society; if industry did not bring with it its reward, and idleness its punishment, the middle parts would not certainly be what they now are.' It was for the same reason that 'the passion between the sexes' was 'necessary' and would remain 'nearly in its present state'. 'The principle, according to which population increases, prevents the vices of mankind, or the accidents of nature, the partial evils arising from general laws, from obstructing the high purpose of the creation.' Such a law could not operate 'without occasioning partial evil'. But evil in this eccentric theodicy was a sort of good: 'Evil exists in the world, not to create despair, but activity.'[50]

Despite its title, Malthus's direct criticism of the social insurance programmes of Condorcet and Paine was cursory. Not more than ten out of nearly 400 pages were devoted to Condorcet's proposals; and in the first edition, Paine was not even mentioned. The treatment was assertive, lacking in detail and, at best, loosely targeted, because it appeared to have been tacked on to an argument devised to refute the differing claims and assumptions of Godwin.

Condorcet – and in the second edition, Paine – presented no theodicy. They could only be conjoined with Godwin insofar as they also subscribed to 'the great error under which Mr Godwin labours throughout his whole work … the attributing almost all the vices and misery that are seen in civil society to human institutions'. Malthus dismissed these institutional causes of misery as 'mere feathers, that float on the surface'.[51]

In other respects, the differences between Godwin and Condorcet or Paine were fundamental. Paine and Condorcet accepted self-interest as the basis of society and government and pushed Adam Smith's 'natural progress of opulence' in an egalitarian direction. They criticised monopolies and excessive concentrations of private property in the land, but not the principle of private property itself. Like Smith, they considered security of property a source of progress and independence. They praised commercial society as an advance upon the feudal past, shared Smith's confidence in capital investment and rejected ascetic and moralistic attitudes towards luxuries. By contrast, Godwin thought private property a source of injustice, dependence, greed and egoism. Like Rousseau and Price, he associated commerce and luxury with inequality and depopulation, and his picture of commercial society was that of Mandeville rather than Smith. Commercial society was, however, only a transient phase in the progress towards a truly egalitarian civilisation, where the main stimulus to activity would be 'love of distinction' and ultimately a purely impersonal love of justice.

According to Malthus, Condorcet's proposals might appear 'very promising upon paper', but 'applied to real life they will be found to be absolutely nugatory'. The provision of cheaper credit institutions for the poor, he believed, would place 'the idle and negligent' on the same footing as 'the active and industrious', and would necessitate 'an inquisition' to examine claims which would be 'little else than a repetition upon a larger scale of the English poor laws'. It would be 'completely destructive of the true principles of liberty and equality'. But these were no more than elaborations of his basic objection: that the existence of a social insurance fund would remove 'the goad of necessity' from 'the labour necessary to procure subsistence for an extended population'. 'Were every man sure of a comfortable provision for a family, almost every man would have one; and were the rising generation free from the "killing frost" of misery, population must readily increase.'[52]

In essence, the attack on Condorcet was little more than the specification of a larger but generally unavowed object of attack, the stance towards labourers adopted by Adam Smith himself. Smith accepted as a truism that 'the demand for men, like that for any other commodity, necessarily regulates the production of men; quickens it when it goes too slowly and stops it when it goes too fast'. But this did not mean that the poor only worked when pushed by 'necessity'. Among the reasons Smith gave for his support for high wages was that the labourer was likely to be encouraged 'by the comfortable hope of bettering his condition'.

'Where wages are high, accordingly, we shall always find the workmen more active, diligent and expeditious, than where they are low.' Conversely, as he argued about the dissenting clergy in *The Wealth of Nations*, 'fear is in almost all cases a wretched instrument of government, and ought in particular never be employed against any order of men who have the smallest pretensions to independency'.[53] Smith never employed the notion of 'indolence' in connection with the labouring poor – this he reserved for depictions of the landed classes and the established clergy.[54]

Condorcet and Paine had only reiterated Smith in expressing their confidence in the natural progress of opulence upon the labourer's hope of bettering his condition. Smith made no reference to the 'goad of necessity', nor did he suggest any essential difference of mentality between rich and poor. On the contrary, he assumed an equality of 'natural talent'. The differences between the philosopher and the street porter were 'much less than we are aware of' and were, for the most part, the effect rather than the cause of the division of labour. Persons from all classes desired respect, 'to be taken notice of with sympathy', to be decently attired and to be able to appear without shame in public.[55]

In Malthus's *Essay* there was a palpable shift. In his opinion, 'the labouring poor, to use a vulgar expression, seem always to live from hand to mouth. Their present wants employ their whole attention, and they seldom think of the future. Even when they have an opportunity of saving, they seldom exercise it; but all that is beyond their present necessities goes generally speaking, to the ale house.' His polemic against the Poor Laws was also premised upon an assumption of the lack of any discernible desire among the poor to preserve their self-respect. The poor who went to the ale house would save and not drink 'if they didn't know they could rely on parish assistance for support in case of accidents'. The labourer would behave differently if he were assured that 'his family must starve, or be left to the support of casual bounty'. Unlike Smith's poor, who were brought within the norms of civil society by sympathy, neighbour-hood, custom and education, Malthus's poor, even when they knew better, were governed by 'their bodily cravings' – 'the cravings of hunger, the love of liquor, the desire of possessing a beautiful woman'.[56]

Soon after the *Essay* originally appeared, clerical friends evidently pointed out to Malthus its unsoundness as an exercise in Christian homiletics. He had ascribed 'misery' not to the Fall and the original 'depravity of man', but to the laws of nature. He had had nothing to say either about the Incarnation or about the Resurrection. Man was made in 'the image of God', how then could he be 'inert' and 'sluggish'? Worse still, Malthus's God, despite his omnipotence and omniscience, apparently made mistakes: 'the works of the Creator', Malthus maintained, were 'not formed with equal perfection'. Finally, in God's cosmic struggle to create mind, imperfect specimens, rather than await the Day of Judgement, appeared to return to 'the inertia of matter': a solution nearer to Seneca than to the New Testament.[57]

In the second edition of the *Essay*, which appeared in 1803, Malthus recast his 'principle of population' along more orthodox Anglican lines. Ideas about the divine process of the creation of mind were replaced by more orthodox conceptions of the world as a state of trial, and by foregrounding the prudential check in the shape of deferred marriage. Malthus's theodicy therefore appeared to converge with the more conventional anti-Jacobin emphasis upon Christianity's capacity to induce restraint. In this way he was also able to produce a Christian conception of an individually attainable way out of poverty and a sustainable improvement in the standard of life for the lower classes. According to Waterman, merely as a result of self-love, individuals defer marriage to achieve 'a *target* income'; this restricts the supply of labour, raises its price and thereby brings about an unintended and beneficent outcome. Marriage and private property turn out to be the most effective institutions in harnessing self-love to the goals of benevolence. [58]

In recent years, historians have also revised the received interpretation of Malthus in other respects.[59] They have emphasised Malthus's moderate reformism and his association of prudence among the lower classes with education and civil and political liberty in the second and subsequent editions of the *Essay*. They have also recognised his achievement as a pioneer in the understanding of the operational constraints of the early modern economy. Malthus himself observed that 'the histories of mankind that we possess, are histories only of the higher classes'; and he argued for enquiries into 'the observable differences in the state of the lower classes of society, with respect to ease and happiness, at different times during a certain period'.[60] According to the foremost historian of English demography, A. E. Wrigley, 'there is now a substantial body of evidence supporting Malthus's view of the relationship between rates of population growth, real wage changes, and the operation of the preventive check during the centuries immediately before his birth'. And this achievement has been underlined by Wrigley's own researches, which have confirmed the reasonableness of the concern, found both in Malthus and in the work of his great contemporary, the political economist David Ricardo, about declining marginal returns to land. As Wrigley explains it,

> The key point is simple. Land was a necessary factor in all forms of material production to a degree not easily recognised in a post-industrial revolution setting. Almost all raw materials were either vegetable or animal: even where mineral raw materials were employed, they were capable of conversion into a useful form only by burning a vegetable fuel. Much the same was also true of the sources of mechanical and heat energy: human and animal muscle and wood fuel were the preponderant means by which raw materials were converted into useful products and transported to places convenient for their subsequent use or consumption. Therefore, the productivity of the land set limits to the scale of industrial activity no less than to

the level of food consumption. Each of these two great consumers of the products of the land was necessarily in competition with the other for the use of a factor of production whose supply could not be expanded.[61]

But however salutary these correctives, they cannot entirely dispel the criticisms his original antagonists directed at Malthus. In the first place, it was not true that Condorcet (or for that matter, Godwin) had not considered the difficulty posed by population. Condorcet believed that if a time were to come when 'the number of men shall surpass the means of their subsistence', that time would be 'extremely distant'. Malthus countered that 'this constantly subsisting cause of periodical misery, has existed ever since we have had any histories of mankind, does exist at present and will for ever continue to exist'. But he never wholly explained why that should be the case when so much of the globe's surface still remained uncultivated. This was Godwin's original response and it was an objection repeated by Hazlitt, Coleridge and Southey whatever the other changes in their subsequent political positions.[62]

Condorcet himself stated that if at some remote point the limits of population might be reached, 'the progress of reason will have kept pace with that of the sciences, and the absurd prejudices of superstition will have ceased to corrupt and degrade the moral code by its harsh doctrine instead of purifying and elevating it' – a veiled reference to contraception, plainly discussed in an unpublished manuscript on the tenth epoch. Malthus referred to Condorcet's removal of the difficulty 'in a manner, which I profess not to understand', while also accusing him of advocating 'promiscuous concubinage' which it was widely believed at the time 'would prevent breeding'. His objection to either of these solutions was moral. 'To remove the difficulty in this way will, surely, in the opinion of most men, be, to destroy that virtue, and purity of manners, which the advocates of equality, and of the perfectibility of man, profess to be the end and object of their views.'[63]

Finally, even if Malthus were correct about the general 'oscillation' between prosperity and indigence produced by the population principle in the early modern world, he did not establish any close correlation between those oscillations in England and the history of the Poor Laws. Despite the existence of these laws since Tudor times, England had increased in prosperity at least after 1688. Malthus himself noted a happy conjuncture between 'character' and 'prudential habits' in the period before 1750. Furthermore, as Malthus was to admit in 1817, the Poor Laws had not lowered the age of marriage.[64]

Historians generally suggest that Malthus 'softened' his position in the second edition of 1803 and adopted a more optimistic assessment of the chances of improvement in the condition of the poor. But this is only half true. On the question of social security and the rights of the poor, Malthus not only adopted a harsher tone, but presented an alarmist, even apocalyptic scenario. For the first time, he discussed Paine's *Rights of Man* which, according to him, had done 'great mischief among the lower and middling classes of people in this country'. After objecting in reasonable terms that Paine underestimated the differences between Britain and America, he attacked Paine's tax proposals, not only as ruinous but as a short path to tyranny, aided by a mob composed of the 'redundant population' – 'of all monsters the most fatal to freedom'. The habit of attributing distress to the nation's rulers or to the character of political institutions, he now considered to be 'the rock of defence, the castle, the guardian spirit of despotism'. Its prevalence was particularly dangerous in a year of near famine prices such as 1800–1. The example of the French Revolution which had 'terminated in military despotism', showed how dangerous it was when 'any dissatisfied man of talents has power to persuade the lower classes of people that all their poverty and distress arise solely from the iniquity of government'.[65]

It was the thought of the 'mischief' done by Paine that led Malthus to assert in far more emphatic and unequivocal terms than anything he had written in the first edition that

> there is one right which man has generally been thought to possess, which I am confident he neither does, nor can possess – a right to subsistence when his labour will not fairly purchase it. Our laws indeed say that he has this right, and bind the society to furnish employment and food to those who cannot get them in the regular market, but in so

doing, they attempt to reverse the laws of nature; and it is in consequence to be expected, not only that they should fail in their object, but that the poor who are intended to be benefited, should suffer most cruelly from this inhuman deceit which is practised upon them.[66]

And he continued the thought in a notorious passage which his opponents never allowed him to forget, even though he withdrew it in the third edition of 1806 and in all subsequent editions:

A man is born into a world already possessed, if he cannot get subsistence from his parents on whom he has a just demand, and if the society do not want his labour, has no claim of *right* to the smallest portion of food, and, in fact, has no business to be where he is. At nature's mighty feast there is no vacant cover for him. She tells him to be gone, and will quickly execute her own orders, if he does not work upon the compassion of some of her guests.[67]

The position adopted by Malthus in important ways exemplified not only how fear of the French Revolution changed the terms of the debate about poverty, but also about the polity as a whole. In the eighteenth century, as Mark Philp has written, the primary fear had been of arbitrary executive rule and the pretensions of the crown.[68] As a result of the Revolution, the crown began to acquire a widespread and unheard-of popularity and something of the respectability it eventually achieved in the Victorian era.[69] At the same time, while the 'mixed constitution' was endowed by Burke with a sanctity which subsequent reform movements came tacitly to accept, there had developed a deeper and more lasting fear of the mobilisation of the masses. Malthus summed up the change quite precisely in 1803:

> As a friend to freedom, and an enemy to large standing armies, it is with extreme reluctance that I am compelled to acknowledge that, had it not been for the organised force in the country, the distresses of the people in the late scarcities, encouraged by the extreme ignorance and folly of many among the higher classes, might have driven them to commit the most dreadful outrages, and ultimately to involve the country in all the horrors of famine … Great as has been the influence of corruption, I cannot yet think so meanly of the country gentlemen of England as to believe that they would thus have given up a part of their birth-right of liberty, if they had not been actuated by a real and genuine fear that it was then in greater danger from the people than from the crown.[70]

In the longer term, the debate on the French Revolution, as Greg Claeys has shown, led to a general retreat from the language of rights on the part of moderate Whigs and the adoption of a language of 'commerce, manners and civili-sation'. Natural rights were henceforth left to the working classes and thoughts of a republic confined to a small minority of ultra radicals.[71] What Malthus added to this basic political shift was a new way of thinking about poverty and inequality, quite as momentous as the proposals of Condorcet, Paine and Godwin, which provoked it, and with far more immediate effect. The poor were no longer those 'ye have ... always with you', a constant presence recalling to us the vanity of earthly ambition and false pride and an unceasing reminder of our duty to practise the Christian duty of charity; the political and cultural significance of Malthus's shift towards an emphasis upon 'prudential restraint' was that poverty could be avoided. But if it could be avoided, it should no longer be condoned. 'Dependent poverty', as Malthus remarked in the first edition of the *Essay*, 'ought to be held digraceful'.[72]

Like Paine, Malthus wished to do away with the existing Poor Laws. Like Godwin, he supported independence of judgement, but 'independence' was no longer counterposed to dependence upon a bloated aristocracy or upon the sinecures, monopolies and vested interests of a corrupt state. It now meant the individual's independence of all forms of parish authority, especially the alleged tyranny of overseers enforcing the Law of Settlement, and the ability to depend upon one's own individual resources.[73] Henceforth, reformers, at least of the 'philosophical' kind, whatever their continuing criticism of the aristocracy or the rich, felt obliged also, or perhaps even primarily, to couple progress with the possibility of overcoming the 'indolence' of the 'working classes'.

John Stuart Mill might claim that only from the time of the 1798 *Essay* 'has the economical condition of the labouring classes been regarded by thoughtful men as susceptible of permanent improvement', but this new awareness came at the cost of projecting on to the 'labouring poor' a new form of moral pedagogy which, not surprisingly, encountered strong resentment.[74] Cobbett and other representatives of the 'working classes' denounced it as a spurious justification for a scheme to remove the *existing* rights of the poor. The presence of a Tory Romantic strand in Chartism becomes more understandable.

Such a scheme proved particularly offensive when harnessed to a new and up-to-date justification of inequality. Inequality was no longer synonymous with a God-ordained hierarchy of ranks, but manmade and thus the result of indolence or economic incompetence. Malthus had no desire to defend the 'present great inequality of property' as 'either necessary or useful to society'. But he only wished to 'prove the necessity of a class of proprietors, and a class of labourers'.[75] In other words, he was not prepared to defend traditional and hierarchical forms of inequality in the manner of Burke, but he was happy to defend the new form of inequality associated with commercial society, and indeed provide divine support for it.

The point was most eloquently put by his disciple and future Archbishop of Canterbury, John Bird Sumner. 'Inequalities of Ranks and Fortunes', argued Sumner in 1816, was the condition best suited to the development of human faculties and to the exercise of virtue. Just as Newton had brought 'the mechanism of the natural world' under the operation of 'a single and universal law', so the moral realm was also subject to 'the operation of a single principle' – the principle of population. According to 'the Design of the Creator', therefore, existence on earth was 'a state of discipline in which the various faculties of mankind are to be exerted and their moral character formed, tried and confirmed, previous to their entering upon a future and higher state ... Life, therefore, is with great propriety described as a race in which a prize is to be contended for.'[76]

III

THE REACTION
IN FRANCE

In France at the beginning of the nineteenth century a separation of political economy from politics similar to that which was occurring in Britain was also declared. In a 'preliminary discourse' preceding his *Traité d'économie politique*, first published in 1803 and destined to become the best-known economic treatise in nineteenth-century France, Jean-Baptiste Say asserted that 'political economy' had too long been confused with 'politics'. Questions about how wealth was formed, distributed and consumed were 'essentially independent of political organisation'. 'Under all forms of government', he went on, 'a state can prosper, if it is well administered.' If there was any connection between wealth and political liberty, it was at best indirect. In making this claim, Say appealed to the authority of Adam Smith. Political economy was now described as a 'natural science' which proceeded from 'general facts' valid in every type of society, while the status of Smith was compared with that of Newton.[1]

Say's assertion was also a product of political defeat.

But of a different kind. It was the result not of intimidation by the loyalist supporters of church and king, but of disappointment with the repeated and unsuccessful efforts to secure the future of the new French republic. In 1802, Say had been expelled from the Tribunate for questioning censorship, along with fifty others. Later in the year, Bonaparte was declared First Consul for life and in 1804, he became Emperor of the French. France had fallen back into the corrupt and bellicose politics of monarchy.

Napoleon triumphed, not over the visionary republic of 1792, but over a dispirited and discredited regime already living under the shadow of military dictatorship. In the early years of the Revolution, there had been a sustained effort to think through and bring about the end of poverty, and even to legislate proposed reforms. Set in this context, the social insurance proposals of Paine and Condorcet had been much less outlandish than they were subsequently to appear.

Poverty, 'indigence' or 'mendicity' had been a pressing concern from the beginning of the Revolution. 1788 and 1789 were years of serious crop failure. Law and order had broken down in many areas, and rumours of the invasion of beggars and brigands had spread from village to village, in what the eminent French Revolutionary historian George Lefèbvre described as 'the Great Fear'. As early as 3 August 1789, a proposal was put to the National Assembly that the government take responsibility for the unemployed. In January 1790 the Comité de Mendicité was established under the energetic chairmanship of the duc de La Roche-foucauld-Liancourt to explore ways to 'destroy mendicity', optimistically regarded as a legacy of the discredited practices of the old regime, and in particular, the church.[2]

During the time of the *ancien régime*, the state had intervened only occasionally, mainly if mendicancy posed a problem of public order, as in the 1760s when a series of so-called *dépôts de mendicité* had been established with the ambition of clearing beggars off the highways and the streets. Locally, intendants might also intervene in the administration of relief. Turgot's time as Intendant of Limoges was remembered particularly for his programme of public works for the unemployed in place of the traditional distribution of alms. Otherwise, as in most Catholic countries, relief of the poor before 1789 fell into the domain of the parish priest – where there was one – and the religious orders. The Catholic attitude, reiterated by luminaries of the Counter-reformation such as Saint Vincent de Paul, had been that the poor were to be accepted as 'the suffering children of Christ'. Just as Christ had washed the feet of the poor, so the constant presence of the poor was an invitation to acts of humility and self-sacrifice on the part of Christians. The poor in this scenario mattered less in themselves as objects of targeted charity; they were rather the means through which the believer might achieve salvation.

After 1715 this Counter-reformation approach came increasingly under attack. While Voltaire and Helvetius publicly questioned the purpose of monks and nuns, Physiocratic theorists attacked the lack of discrimination and inefficiency of charitable relief. In his contributions to the Encyclopaedia, Turgot argued that most charities subsidised laziness and diminished the productive capacity of the country. Others criticised the local *curé*'s control over the distribution of parochial relief, with its opportunities for favouritism and preference for the '*pauvres honteux*' (the shame-faced poor), those of impeccable piety who had fallen from a more genteel status. Such criticism coincided with the beginnings of a more secular understanding of poverty as an effect of social and economic change, but also with increasingly frequent waves of panic about the importunity and the pervasive threat of violence associated with roaming beggars.[3]

The Comité de Mendicité initiated a systematic enquiry into the extent of poverty across France and discovered that beggars amounted to 1,928,064 out of a total population of 16,634,466, or one in eight of the population. La Rochefoucauld-Liancourt and his committee set out a new set of assumptions which were to guide policy through to the summer of 1794. Charity, he argued, was inefficient, condescending and outmoded. Poverty was an inescapable consequence of a society based upon inequality and subject to economic change. The term charity – the discretionary giving on the part of individuals, primarily for religious motives – should be replaced by the national obligation to provide *bienfaisance* (beneficence) as a right. As a report to the Legislative Assembly in 1792 put it, 'Every man has the right to subsistence through work, if he is able-bodied, and to free assistance if he is unable to work.' Assistance previously regarded 'as a favour rather than a duty' should now be considered 'a national responsibility'. The reasons were as much social as political. Destitution was the cause of the violent crime which terrorised the countryside; it was also detrimental to liberty since it encouraged an inappropriate attitude of submissiveness among the citizenry.[4]

The committee believed that it was not sufficient to relieve poverty: 'It is no doubt an imperative duty to assist poverty, but that of preventing it is no less sacred or necessary.' It would therefore be necessary, the committee argued, to create public savings institutions, based upon 'the calculation of probabilities, of chances and of the accumulation of interest'. Until then, such calculation had scarcely been employed except to assist lotteries which were harmful to the people. 'No establishment, no instruction makes clear to that useful and working class how it could apply these calculations to its advantage or furnishes the means to do it.' The example of private companies in other countries was rejected since the deduction of returns to shareholders and administrative costs were too high, meaning that benefits were too low. Therefore, the organisation of foresight (*prévoyance*) like that of 'benificence' should become the responsibility of the state. In each *département* there would be created a savings bank whose costs were to be as low as possible.[5]

Particular importance, as in Paine's proposals, was

attached to the problems of working families overburdened with the support of 'excess' offspring. Under the *ancien régime*, the problem of abandoned infants had been acute. Whether received in foundling hospitals or put out to nurse, the chances of survival of these children were appallingly low. While suggesting better institutions for foundlings, the report of 1792 argued that abandonment could largely be prevented by the state providing home relief for the children of poor families. It was similarly argued that the elderly and the infirm should be awarded annual cash pensions rather than the weekly distribution of aid in kind.

Later, the far less visible problem of rural poverty was also addressed. In May 1794, Barère, one of the most prominent members of the notorious Committee for Public Safety during the period of terror, introduced legislation to provide pensions to aged farm workers and rural artisans, indigent mothers and widows. Pressed by the need to preserve the morale of a war-torn population, the Jacobins decreed that these neglected groups were to be treated with the same respect as wounded soldiers and war widows. Such pensions were to be disbursed in communes with populations less than 3,000 and provided, not as a gift, but as a recompense for work.[6]

Historians have not found it difficult to demonstrate that the real impact of these policies upon the poor was small. Apart from a decree authorising the expenditure of 15 million livres on emergency public work programmes, La Rochefoucauld-Liancourt's Comité de Mendicité was forced to wind up its proceedings in September 1791 before it could introduce significant legislation. The successor committee in the Legislative Assembly was also cut short by the fall of the monarchy in August 1792. It was not therefore until the sitting of the Convention in 1793 and the appointment of its Committee on Public Assistance that major legislation pledging pensions to aged and infirm indigents and allowances to poor families was adopted, in the law of 28 June 1793. Furthermore, although an administrative framework for the central funding of *bienfaisance* and a coherent formula for its local distribution were carefully worked out, what was no more than the first instalment of actual funds, 10 million livres, was not authorised by the Convention until February 1794; and no further instalments were forthcoming. Not surprisingly, by 1794, bitterness and cynicism were setting in. A police spy recorded a Parisian munitions worker as stating: 'We're dying of hunger and they mock us with pretty speeches.'[7]

Barère's proposals were implemented, but it was only a matter of months before the value of these pensions had been all but wiped out. Seventeen ninety-five was a terrible disaster both for the Revolution and for the poor. Due to the flight or evasion of the rich, tax receipts were already declining before the fall of Robespierre on 27 July 1794. Hyperinflation in the following year brought about the collapse of the currency. The *assignat* (the new form of paper currency introduced in the French Revolution and originally set against the value of church land), which still traded at one-third of its value in July 1794, had fallen to 1 per cent of its stated value by the end of 1795.

This in turn meant the virtual bankruptcy of the state. The large scheme for state-financed primary education ground to a halt, since there were no funds from which to pay teachers' salaries. At the same time, the winter of 1794–5 was the worst since 1709. Suicides and deaths from starvation reached unheard-of peaks. Tragically, also, the crisis struck not long after the nursing sisters (usually nuns) who staffed the hospitals had been sacked. Most hospitals and municipal charities, already hit by the abolition of feudal dues, had been stripped of their independent endowments. Following the decree of 11 July 1794, all charitable property was to be sold off and the proceeds transferred to the state.

The revolutionary policy of *bienfaisance* was not as misguided as it was subsequently to appear. As Alan Forrest has written, '[I]n the early years of the Revolution, before the money ran out and other priorities became too insistent to be denied, the cash grants to hospitals and local councils did seem to be providing a standard of care to the old and the sick and a level of pension to the deserving poor that far surpassed the product of the random charities and legacies of the eighteenth century.'[8] Local studies of the implementation of such schemes, particularly in Paris, also suggest that, even in the adverse conditions of 1794–5, the new organisation of relief could be thorough and efficient.[9]

But in the harsh and confused conditions of France after the fall of Robespierre, contemporaries did not make fine discriminations in deciding what had gone wrong with the policy of *bienfaisance*. In the face of a bankrupt treasury and a population struggling to survive the chaos of grain shortages and hyper-inflation, there was a headlong retreat from the notion of collective political responsibility for the problem of poverty. The supporters of the post-Jacobin Thermidorian regime (1794–1802) rationalised this stance by attributing the failure of *bienfaisance* to Jacobin mega-lomania and 'a mania for levelling', which they claimed had also been responsible for the drying-up of private charity. In late 1796, the government halted the sale of hospital and charitable property, repealed all the public assistance laws of 1793–4 and cancelled all pension entitlements except those of veterans and war widows. The rural poor were once again largely left to their fate. In Paris and other large towns, in place of direct taxation, relief was once again funded by entertainment and excise taxes – a return to the methods of the *ancien régime*.

But although the Terror had come to an end, revolution-ary *bienfaisance* had been phased out and Robespierre's cult of the Supreme Being discontinued, the Revolution was not over. There was to be no return to the Bourbon monarchy, no restitution of church property and no rehabilitation of Christianity itself. The events of the preceding six years had resulted in France becoming a secular republic, now com-mitted to a republican rather than a Christian morality. How, within this unanticipated and unfamiliar framework, was the problem of poverty now to be addressed?

At first, the Thermidorian republic still seemed to be committed to the hopes of 1792. In 1795 it ordered 3,000 copies of Condorcet's *Sketch* be published at its own expense. But Condorcet's vision of the reduction of inequality and the elimination of poverty was well beyond both the capacity and the will of the post-Thermidorian state. More akin to the policies of the ruling Directorate was a strand of Girondin thinking which located the solution to poverty in a reform of manners rather than in the schemes of collective provision associated with Condorcet and Paine. This form of republicanism had also looked to the new American republic for its inspiration, but with quite different results.

The treatment of wealth and poverty in Say's 1803 *Treatise on Political Economy* was a product of this line of thinking. In histories of economic thought, Say's contribution to political economy has conventionally been interpreted as the emergence of a 'Smithian', or anti-Physiocratic, school in France. But although Say's use of Smith was conspicuous and extensive, the fervent and optimistic hopes which Say invested in 'industriousness' (*industrie*) and 'frugality' (*frugalité*) as the answer to want (*misère*) cannot really be attributed to Smith. They can only be understood as the reformulation of an answer to a question Smith had no occasion to ask. How could the vicious and corrupt ethos created by the monarchy and priesthood of the *ancien régime* be supplanted by the formation of a set of manners and beliefs which would ensure the survival of the new French republic? Or, to put the question in the words employed by

Say himself in 1797 in a prize essay written six years before the appearance of his *Treatise*, by what means can one ensure that 'a people grown old in vicious habits and deadly prejudices might follow those rules by whose observation happiness would be the infallible reward'?[10]

Much of the political and economic reasoning under-pinning the strand of republicanism from which Say emerged originated in the circle formed in the 1780s around the Genevan financier Étienne Clavière, later to be champion of the *assignat* and Minister of Finance in 1792. Say, also a Genevan from a mercantile background, had joined Clavière's pension insurance firm as a clerk in 1785 and from 1787 to 1792 had worked as his secretary.[11] Clavière had been one of the leaders of the Democratic Party in Geneva until forced into exile in 1782. His Genevan experience led him to associate egoism, luxury and idleness with aristocratic rule. Convinced by England's success in the Seven Years' War that the legal despotism of the Phys-iocrats would not provide the best means of transforming France, in the 1780s Clavière, together with his close allies (and commissioned writers) Brissot and Mirabeau, came to believe that commerce could provide the solvent to weaken France's rigid hierarchy of ranks and undermine the privi-leges of the nobility. Turgot had also encouraged radicals to think in terms of the similarities between a reformed France and North America rather than the mixed constitu-tion of Britain. Finally, in a move away from the received doctrine of both Rousseau and Montesquieu, the Clavière circle also came to believe that a republic was possible in a large and developed state like France. The reason for this shift in position was, of course, the success of the American Revolution and the enthusiasm the new republic generated among reforming circles in Paris.

The reform programme of the future Girondins therefore began to coalesce around commercial development, a popular legislative assembly and legislation to encourage the formation of republican manners. The strong emphasis upon the fundamental importance of manners found among the Clavière circle (perhaps in origin the legacy of another Genevan, Rousseau) was greatly reinforced and powerfully shaped by the reading of Richard Price's 1784 *Observations on the Importance of the American Revolution*, immediately translated by Mirabeau into French. Price considered that the American Revolution was second in importance only to the introduction of Christianity in the progressive course of the 'improvement' of mankind. His depiction of the manners of the Americans became the political and social ideal which the Clavière circle aimed to turn into reality in a renewed republican France.

According to Price,

the happiest state of man is the middle state between the savage and the refined, or between the wild and the luxurious state. Such is the state of society in Connecticut and some others of the American provinces where the inhabitants consist, if I am rightly informed, of an independent and hardy yoemanry, nearly all on a level, trained to arms, instructed in their rights, clothed in homespun, of simple manners, strangers to luxury, drawing plenty from the ground, and that plenty gathered easily by the hand of industry and giving rise to early marriages, a numerous progeny, length of days, and a rapid increase – the rich and the poor, the haughty grandee and the creeping sycophant, equally unknown – protected by laws which (being their own will) cannot oppress, and by an equal government which, wanting lucrative places, cannot create corrupt canvassings and ambitious intrigue.[12]

It was imperative, Price thought, for America to preserve this state of equality. But if it were to do so, it was also necessary to guard against three 'enemies'. These were: firstly, hereditary honours and titles of nobility; secondly, primogeniture; and lastly, foreign trade. Price feared 'an increasing fashion for foreign frippery', bringing back with it 'effeminacy, servility and venality'. He therefore suggested a 'heavy duty on importations'.[13]

In 1789, faced with the debt crisis of the French crown, Clavière, like other speculators who handled government loans, was eager to avoid the demand for a state bankruptcy, found in so many of the *Cahiers de doléances* of 1789. He also opposed the introduction of income tax or a land tax, together with the establishment of a national bank proposed respectively by Condorcet and Dupont de Nemours. Instead, Clavière argued that credit could be stabilised by the extension of the use of *assignats* as a paper currency guaranteed by the state's appropriation of church lands.

Despite, or perhaps because of, his own involvement in the insurance industry, Clavière did not support the social insurance schemes of Paine and Condorcet. He argued instead that the *assignats* could also form the basis of a social policy designed to promote frugality, industriousness and the growth of republican manners. He defended himself against Condorcet's charge that thrift was being ruined by the falling value of the *assignat* by blaming its decline upon the agents of Pitt. But even Clavière's confidence in the *assignats* waned in the course of 1792, during which the currency fell to 50 per cent of its nominal value. In June of the following year, he was arrested along with other Girondins and only averted death by guillotine by committing suicide on 9 December 1793.

Say escaped this fate because in August 1792 he had volunteered for the army and remained out of the reach of the Jacobins when he returned to Paris in May 1793. From April 1794, he edited *La Décade*, which became the journal in which debates among those who had survived from 'the party of philosophy' found their most congenial home.[14]

Somewhat against expectation, the Revolution had survived the end of the Terror, but the new republic now sailed in uncharted seas and its survival remained in constant doubt. Although Thermidorians emphasised their constitutionality and rejection of the Terror, it was only by tampering with election results and calling in the army that they managed to cling on to power. The threat came from both the left and the right. Even after the failed Babeuf 'Conspiracy of the Equals' of 1796, Jacobins plotted a return to power. But more formidable was the threat from Catholics and royalists. For following the separation of church and state and the re-opening of the churches in 1795, it became clear that the loyalty of the majority of the population in large parts of France was still to the church rather than to the new republic. Royalists scoffed that France was a republic without republicans, while Thermidorians feared that the return of the monarchy would soon follow that of recalcitrant priests.

How could a republic be established in a nation whose habits and beliefs remained so deeply corrupted by the legacy of monarchy and church? Say's answer to this Thermidorian question was that the long-term survival of the Republic depended upon a drastic transformation of manners. He believed that this could of itself overcome poverty, inequality and egoism. Others argued that what was needed was a new *pouvoir spirituel*, or spiritual power, to replace that of the church. Say denied the need for a new religion, but believed that a purely secular morality could operate in its place. And so it was that the industriousness and frugality, so glowingly described in the Unitarian preacher Richard Price's evocation of the American republic, became for Say the centrepiece of a new republican ethic.

Say had already indicated the basis of his approach by publishing in 1794 a translation of Benjamin Franklin's *Poor*

Richard's Almanack of 1733–58 under the title *La Science du bonhomme Richard*. The kernel of Franklin's message was best summed up in the 1758 address of 'Father Abraham' in response to complaints about 'the Badness of the Times' and the heaviness of taxes. After an initial reluctance and the observation that 'many words won't fill a bushel', he proceeded:

> Friends … and Neighbours, the Taxes are indeed very heavy, and if those laid on by the Government were the only Ones we had to pay, we might more easily discharge them; but we have many others, and much more grievous to some of us. We are taxed twice as much by our *Idleness*, three times as much by our *Pride*, and four times as much by our *Folly*, and from these Taxes the Commissioners cannot ease or deliver us by allowing an Abatement. However let us hearken to good Advice, and something may be done for us; *God helps them that help themselves.*[15]

According to Say, Franklin was 'one of the greatest triumphs of equality … that has opened our eyes, and prepared the establishment of our august Republic'.[16]

The manners required to ensure the survival of the Republic were spelled out in Say's essay *Olbie or an Essay on the Means to Reform the Manners of a Nation*. As in the schemes of Paine, Condorcet and the Comité de Mendicité, the elimination of poverty, as of excessive wealth, was a priority above all because it represented a political danger.

Poverty exposed the people to temptation and bred violence. Deceit, cheating, prostitution and riot were almost always the products of indigence. Great riches bred 'idleness' and 'the train of vices which accompany it'.[17]

In Olbie, however, lived a fictional people not unlike the French but portrayed as they would be fifty years after their revolution, their manners resembling those of Price's Americans. In Olbie, the majority of inhabitants enjoyed an 'honest affluence'(honnête aisance); indigence or excessive opulence were rare. No longer were there to be seen 'taverns full of brutalised drunks singing or swearing'. Instead, the majority of Olbians found pleasure in the society of their family and friends; and parents and children were often to be encountered walking in the countryside which surrounded the town. There were no lotteries in Olbie, no books on magic or necromancy. Olbians loved work, but not primarily for the sake of gain; and they were protected from poverty in sickness or old age by their regular contributions to savings banks. Conspicuous consumption no longer attracted admiration. The heads of the Olbian state had adopted a general style of simplicity, in their clothes, their pleasures and their social relations. Olbians consumed nothing beyond what was truly necessary for their use or enjoyment. As a result, 'luxury' had been attacked at its root by 'opinion', and had given way to a more widely distributed 'affluence'. The extra resources of the wealthy were now deployed in more productive directions.[18]

How had this revolution in manners taken place? Price

and others had already observed that peoples transposed into new environments adopted new habits. The Europeans who had sailed to America had left behind their old patterns of behaviour and even 'the scoundrels' who had been transported to the British penal settlement at Botany Bay had become honest men. In the case of the Olbians, such changes had been accomplished, not by force or terror, but by changes in upbringing and education reinforced by legislation and the establishment of new institutions.[19]

Say did not rule out taxation as a means of promoting equality, but placed most emphasis upon the upbringing of children. He agreed with Rousseau that a people which had learnt good habits needed few laws; as the example of Sparta under Lycurgus showed, 'men are what one makes them'. Most important in this respect was the fact that the Olbians had abandoned Christianity and every other form of religion. Religions had not improved the manners of the human race and Christianity in particular, ostensibly the most peaceful of religions, offered more examples of intolerance and ferocity than all the others. Say believed that fear of disgrace was more powerful in promoting morality than the terrors of hellfire; and as for rewards, in an aside worthy of Fourier, he remarked that he found it difficult to believe that the bliss of encountering God face to face had produced a single good deed. Doing good was not the essential point of religion, but rather adherence to the dogma, the faith, to the sect and its rites. It was not religion but philosophy which had brought about an improvement of manners in

Europe, and it had done so by weakening the power of religious sentiment.[20]

In place of religion the morals of the Olbians were shaped by a book of political economy. 'A good treatise on political economy', wrote Say, 'must be the first book of morality.' 'He who is capable of producing an elementary treatise on political economy, suitable for schools, understood by most subordinate functionaries, by country people and artisans would be a benefactor of his country.'[21]

Knowledge of political economy at all levels of society was reinforced through an education in which the Olbians learnt that self-interest, once enlightened, was identical with virtue, and that the happiness of the self entailed the furthering of the happiness of others. It was also reinforced through the educative effects of monuments, festivals and prizes and the use of various shaming devices to discourage the idle. Prizes for virtue would be awarded at festivals by 'guardians of manners', while any idle person who refused to engage in useful and productive activity would be labelled '*un homme inutile*' ('a useless man'). The sexes would intermingle less in Olbie. Single women would be provided with communal lodgings, perhaps modelled on the Beguinages, where their chastity would be protected. They would no longer be brutalised by coarse work, beings in petticoats with brazen look and raucous voice, who for Say, constituted a 'third sex'.[22]

Lastly, Say repeated Price's warnings about the dangers of foreign commerce and the 'luxury' and corruption which might accompany it. The love of gain was nearly as dangerous as unproductive idleness. The case of the English showed that where monetary resources become immense and their procurement becomes the first concern, the politics of that nation become narrow, exclusive, barbarous and perfidious. Among certain commercial peoples, all ideas other than self-enrichment were regarded as forms of madness. Such were the Phoenicians and Carthaginians in the ancient world, and the Dutch and Venetians in modern times. Even the Americans were not free from such a temptation. Say warned, '[I]f what is said about you is true, you will become rich, but you will not remain virtuous and you will not for long be independent and free.' Such nations might be able to pay to import men of talent, but they were no longer able to produce them.[23]

The distance between *Olbie* and the *Treatise on Political Economy* which Say published three years later in 1803 was less than it may at first seem. Say was still committed to the diminution of inequality. Even in the advanced states of Europe, he estimated that only one person in a thousand enjoyed the 'honest ease' that should be within the reach of all. He still believed that 'luxury' destroyed values, brought poverty in its train and ought to be cut back through taxation. The focus on 'industriousness' and 'frugality' remained central, even if it was now linked more precisely to productive investment and decked out with more elaborate economic arguments taken from Smith. While no longer specifically republican, Say's political economy still presupposed the French Revolution. It started from the Abbé Sieyès's premise in *What is the Third Estate?* that the nation was composed of those who worked, with the strong implication that the aristocracy and the priesthood belonged to an idle and useless class. Smith's *Wealth of Nations* was treated as if it shared a similar vision.[24]

Despite all this, however, Say's attempt to separate political economy from politics did mark a significant step in the process through which political economy came to be viewed as an apology for existing property relations.[25] Industriousness and frugality were no longer seen as attributes of citizenship, since Say had already come to agree with many of the leading Thermidorians that the franchise must be restricted on grounds of political safety. The republican preoccupation with education was similarly omitted. Smith's conception of political economy as 'the science of the legislator' was rejected. In a state possessing representative government, political economy was declared to be everyone's business. But although Say lamented the extent of ignorance of such matters across Europe, he no longer suggested any institutional remedy. Philosophers and legislators were no longer entrusted with a distinctive pedagogical role; enlightenment now spread outwards from the middle class.[26] Similarly, the argument for *laisser faire* was no longer explicitly connected with the process of dismantling the warlike, aristocratic or feudal state. The way was now open to the Romantic and socialist denunciation of *laisser faire* as the ultimate expression of the selfish individualism of the bourgeois.

Lastly, and most immediately relevant, the elimination of poverty was no longer treated as a specifically political concern. As in *Olbie*, Say placed a very great emphasis upon the use of savings banks by workers. To save in this fashion should be as essential and habitual as paying the rent, and if this meant the need for somewhat higher wages, then that was to be encouraged. But Say made no reference to the proposals of Condorcet or Paine, nor even to the more modest proposals made by the Comité de Mendicité, for treasury support of local savings banks in order to bring down the high administrative costs charged by private associations. Instead, Say noted the success of certain private associations in England, Holland and Germany, 'especially where the government has been wise enough not to get mixed up in it' ... 'for a government is too powerful a book-keeper [*comptable*] to inspire full confidence'.[27]

But simply to focus upon the *Treatise* as a closure or submerging of republican concerns would be to miss its powerful effect in transforming the debate about the modern economy and its international ramifications in the years after the battle of Waterloo and the return of the Bourbon king. By removing the discussion of *industrie* from a specifically republican framework, and by rejecting the conjoining of politics and political economy as an obsolete legacy of the ancients, Say directed attention to the centrality and global emancipatory promise of a modern economy based upon the freedom and independence of labour. In this respect, his work was a direct inspiration of the 'industrialism' of

Saint-Simon and indirectly of the delineation of the essential features of modern industrial capitalism – again, irrespective of the particular political character of particular states – found in Marx.[28] More immediately, by connecting his concept of *industrie* to productive capital in the shape of machinery, he was the first, as will be seen in the next chapter, to arrive at the idea of an 'industrial revolution'. He arrived at this new idea, however, in the middle of a new debate about the global features of the new economy and the emergence of the claim that *industrie*, far from being the answer to poverty, was its most powerful progenitor in a new and more ominous form.

IV

GLOBALISATION: THE 'PROLETARIAT' AND THE 'INDUSTRIAL REVOLUTION'

In the years after the battle of Waterloo, discussion of the extraordinary development of the textile industry in Britain and what became known as 'the machinery question' became commonplace in both France and Britain.[1] In France, liberals celebrated the advent of modern industry as a likely bulwark against the opposed forces of feudalism, corporate regulation and protection. In Britain, on the other hand, interest in the possibilities of machinery was overshadowed by Malthusian anxieties about population increase and Ricardian fears about diminishing returns, dramatised by the growth of pauperism and the prohibitive level of agricultural protection afforded by the 1815 Corn Law. The main concern of the defenders of industry was to ward off attack from a mixed collection of conservatives, romantics and visionaries, ranging from Southey through Malthus to Owen, whose one point of convergence was the belief that modern industry – steam power and the growth of factory employment in the textile districts – posed special and unprecedented problems. At least until the 1830s, most liberals and radicals considered such preoccupations as unwelcome diversions from the battle against protectionism, aristocratic power and the fiscal iniquities of the Hanoverian state.

In France, discussion of the 'British case' was sharpened by French defeat in the Napoleonic wars. The earliest and most interesting assessment was a first-hand report, once again by Say, who was commissioned by the government of Louis XVIII to make a fact-finding visit to England in 1814. Say had become famous both as a political economist and as an opponent of Bonaparte. His *Traité d'économie politique* (*Treatise on Political Economy*) of 1803 established him as the foremost European champion of Adam Smith's system of commercial liberty against the agriculturally oriented economics of Physiocracy.

The debate about Physiocracy in France was as much political as economic, and for this reason Say's rejection of Physiocratic theory was more pointed and less equivocal than anything found in Smith. While Smith still conceded a special productiveness to agriculture, in contrast to manufacture where 'nature does nothing for man',[2] Say merged agriculture, manufacture and commerce within a composite notion of '*industrie*'. Nothing distinguished capital invested in agriculture from 'capital employed in utilising any of the productive forces of nature'. Furthermore, from the viewpoint of political economy, what mattered about production was not the creation or transformation of matter, but the creation of utility.

These were not simply technical improvements in economic analysis. Say's argument contained a new political vision of society.[3] *Industrie* was the sole legitimate activity in modern society, and the '*industrieux*' – the '*savants*', '*entrepreneurs*' and '*ouvriers*' associated with the process of production – were its sole legitimate members. Say's *industrieux* were an economic specification of Sieyès' revolutionary conception of the nation, the 'Third Estate', those who worked.[4] They were counterpoised against the '*oisifs*', the idle non-working landowners and *rentiers* whose property was the residue of conquest or occupation.

It was partly to widen the moral and economic breach between those who worked and those who did not that Say introduced his notion of the 'entrepreneur'. Mobilising investment and initiating production were sharply to be distinguished from the mere ownership of stock, even though all these components had been included without discrimination in Smith's conception of capital.[5] But *industrie* was also an extension of what eighteenth-century writers had understood by '*doux commerce*'.[6] Peaceful productive activity linked together the interdependent parts of society, just as *doux commerce* underpinned an emerging world of peaceful commercial exchange. War and exploitation, poverty and unemployment were the residues of a traditional aristocratic global order based upon conquest, violence, corporate privilege and protective tariffs. 'Say's law' – the denial of the possibility of general gluts – presupposed the harmony and complementarity of the international market once institutional barriers were removed.

It is not surprising that Say's vision of peaceful and untrammelled commercial exchange displacing conquest and force did not please Napoleon. When changes were demanded for a second edition of the 1803 *Traité*, Say refused to comply. Under the First Empire, he published nothing more, devoting himself instead to the establishment of a cotton spinning factory in Normandy. Soon after Napoleon's fall in 1814, however, a second, substantially revised edition of the *Traité* appeared. It set the terms not only of the liberal opposition to Buonapartism, but also of the liberal economic case against the protectionist and paternalist proclivities of the returning Bourbons.

To reinforce this position, Say added a new chapter to the 1814 edition of the *Traité*, 'Of the Independence Born out of the Progress of Industry among the Moderns'. This brief distinction between the ancient and modern economies can be compared with Constant's comparison between ancient and modern liberty a few years later.[7] In ancient Rome, Say argued, there was little capital invested in commerce and manufacture, not only because of a shortage of capital, but also because the free citizens, who cultivated land either by themselves or using slaves, held these occupations in low esteem. A large part of the Roman population, the plebs, were thus left without land, capital or wages ('*revenus industriels*'), 'hence the unrest and turbulence of the non-proprietors', the debts which were never redeemed and the trafficking in votes. 'What a poor figure, these masters of the world cut, when they were not in the army or in revolt. They fell into poverty the moment they had no one more to pillage. It was from such people that the clientelage of a Marius, a Sulla, a Pompey, a Caesar, an Anthony or an Augustus were formed.' In the end, the whole Roman people had formed 'the court' of Caligula, Heliogabalus or other monsters who both opposed it and yet were forced to feed it.

Among the moderns all this had changed. Whatever the form of government, every man who possessed an 'industrial talent' was independent. The great were not as rich and powerful as they had been among the ancients. Wars no longer meant plunder of the land and possessions of a defeated people. Such a people was not destroyed, only its government was changed. A conquered nation might be forced to pay a tribute, but this would barely cover the costs of its administration and defence. Similarly, in a modern nation, there was little profit in serving the great, much more in serving the public. The time of clientelage was past. 'The poorest citizen can do without a patron. He begins to entrust himself to the protection of his talent to make a living … Thus modern nations, able to exist wholly by themselves, remain in virtually the same condition when their governments are overthrown.'[8]

Say's notion of *industrie* was concerned with the unimpeded progress of industriousness, peaceful activity, liberal institutions and the march of the mind, not with the level or character of technology. There is therefore no immediate overlap between the *industrie* of French liberals or the St Simonians and 'the industrial revolution' of modern economic historians. Nevertheless, the politics of *industrie* could not but engender a positive stance towards the phenomenon of industrialisation.[9] For industrialism was virtually defined by the belief that problems of inequality and ignorance, poverty and unemployment, were legacies of a feudal, military and aristocratic past. These social ills were the residues of force and fraud or of evil government, not the novel and unanticipated consequences of the progress of invention within the world of industry itself.

Say's pamphlet, translated into English in 1816 as *England and the English People*, is interesting not only for its picture of industrial progress in Britain since 1789, but also for its attempts to explain British economic success.[10] What is striking about Say's picture is that industrialisation was not presented as the result of the excellence of Anglo-Saxon liberal institutions (the jury system, freedom of the press, etc.), but as a by-product of the attempt by its unhappy people to escape the harshness of its taxes and the corruption of its financial management. Say began by noting that England's pre-eminence was not the result of military power, but of wealth and credit, a product of the strength of the 'whole economy'. During the war, while Bonaparte's conquests had turned the whole of Europe into an enemy of

France, English control of the seaways and its ability to sub-
sidise continental allies had ensured a prodigious increase
in its commerce and industry. The population of the towns
had greatly increased and this had in turn benefited farmers
and landholders. According to Say, however, these gains had
been of little profit to the English people:

> But while war animated English industry to … extraor-
> dinary exertions, they produced but little profit to the
> people themselves. Taxes and loans ravished from them
> all its fruits. The taxes bore at once on the productions
> of all classes and took from them the most visible and
> certain proportion of their profits; and the loans absorbed
> the savings of those great dealers and speculators, whose
> situations enabled them to make the best advantage of
> circumstances.[11]

Say went on to detail the huge defence budget and the
amount paid out in sinecures and pensions. It was this
pattern of expenditure which had resulted in the alarming
increase in the national debt from around £1 million in 1689
to £780 million in 1815. Adding interest payment to current
expenses, Say estimated that 'government consumes one
half of the income produced by the soil, the capital, and the
industry of the English people'.[12]

These charges in turn made English goods expensive.
They increased the cost of living for those on fixed incomes
and were 'the cause of the distress of the class of manual

labourers'. It meant that the English nation was 'compelled to perpetual labour'. There were 'no coffee houses, no billiard rooms filled with idlers from morning to night … There everybody runs, absorbed in his own affairs. Those who allow themselves the smallest relaxation from their labours, are promptly overtaken by ruin.' Furthermore, consumption was curtailed, quality was adulterated, advertising was pushed to extremes and serious reading was in decline. Finally, crime – more widespread and frequent in Britain than anywhere else in Europe – increased from year to year in line with taxes and the national debt. Its main cause was 'the economical state of a people' whose 'wants' were 'great in comparison with the means of satisfying them'.[13] But Say went on to concede that 'the necessity of saving on all charges of production' had also produced 'some good effects among many bad ones'. It had led to a perfecting of 'the art of producing', with striking economies of scale to be found, whether in the provision of cheap milk or in the invention of the Lancaster system for the mass education of the poor. In particular, it had resulted in 'the introduction of machinery in the arts' which had 'rendered the production of wealth more economical'.[14] Say noted the widespread use of threshing machines on large farms, but especially of the steam engine, 'the most advantageous substitute for human labour, which the dearness of articles of consumption has made so expensive'. He continued:

There is no kind of work which these machines have not

been made to perform. They spin and weave cotton and wool; they brew beer, and they cut glass. I have seen some which embroider muslin, and churn butter. At Newcastle and at Leeds, walking steam engines draw after them waggons of coal; and nothing more surprises a traveller at first sight, than to meet in the country these long convoys, which proceed by themselves, and without the assistance of any living creature.[15]

Say marvelled at the increase that had occurred in the use of steam during the war. Thirty years before, there had only been two or three steam engines in London; now there were 'thousands' and 'hundreds' in the great manufacturing towns. They were even to be seen 'in the fields', while 'works of industry can no longer be carried on advantageously without them'. Given a plentiful supply of coal 'which nature appears to have placed in reserve to supply the waste of forests … the inevitable result of civilisation', it was possible to foresee the future pattern of industry: 'By the aid of a simple mineralogical chart, a chart of British industry may be formed. There is industry wherever there is coal.'[16]

The problems Britain faced were not caused by industry, but by the ruinous level of its taxes and tariff barriers. The recent introduction of the Corn Law in order to maintain the high price of grain reached during the years of the war was likely to have adverse effects upon export prices. 'The alternative is terrible. Either agriculture and the landholders are ruined if corn does not rise in price, or, if it does, then commerce and manufactures will be destroyed.'[17] Moreover, an even worse problem loomed if the British state continued to maintain its present level of expenditure:

> What would be said of a great landholder, possessing great activity and industry, who, by means of his land and the buildings with which he had enriched it, enjoyed an income of 170,000 francs, but who had had the misfortune of marrying an extravagant wife, who spent for him 260,000 a year; so that this poor husband, notwithstanding his genius and his incessant labour, is obliged to borrow 90,000 francs *per annum* to support his expenses? This is the state of England: I have only taken off four zeros.[18]

The only immediate alternatives were either to continue to borrow and experience increasing difficulty in meeting interest payments or to declare a national bankruptcy, at which point the whole political system would fall. But the only real remedy would be to lessen expenditure 'by ceasing to embroil and agitate Europe, Asia and America'. Britain's military expenditure, greater than that of any other nation, had only been sustained by an 'industry prodigiously active'. But much of that expenditure was pointless. America as an independent country had proved much more profitable to England than it had as a colony. Conversely, the expenses of conquering India outweighed the profits to be derived from it.[19] The lessons to be drawn internationally were the same as those which applied locally. In both cases force and fraud were no substitute for industry. In the course of the nineteenth century, Say prophesied, 'the old colonial system will fall to the ground', since 'sovereignty does not compel a people to buy what they cannot pay for, or what is not suited to their customs; and when they are offered what is agreeable to them, they buy it without being conquered'.[20]

Say's account set out clearly the basic components of a radical or republican diagnosis of Britain's post-war problems. Other French commentators were less pro-grammatic and even more hostile – not surprisingly in the immediate aftermath of the defeat at Waterloo, the loss of much of France's commercial and maritime empire and the dumping of British goods in European markets.[21] An empire based on territory had been defeated by an empire based on trade. Analysis therefore tended to latch on to any sign that 'Carthage' was heading for collapse. The aspects of Britain which most captured the attention of the French were the national debt, the growth of population, the rise of pauperism and the dangers attendant upon British com-mercial and manufacturing superiority.

It was in this context that increasing attention was drawn to the connection between machinery and unem-ployment in the manufacturing districts. In one compendi-ous survey of the situation of England 'on January 1st 1816', the economic journalist and statistician Montvéran noted that the adoption of machinery had been of great assistance to manufacturers during the period between 1802 and 1808, but thereafter increasingly harmful:

> First of all, the machines left a multitude of hands without work; then, through the help of its steam-powered machinery or water power or other natural forces, a reduced number of workers produced much more, far beyond the needs of general consumption; objects manufactured in too large a quantity fell in price and tended constantly to cheapen in the markets of the world; they had to be sold at great loss and although this loss was divided between several classes of producers and merchants, it was no less real or substantial for the mass of English commerce.[22]

But despite these dangers France had no alternative but to follow England's lead in the development of cotton textiles. According to Napoleon's ex-Director of Commerce, Agriculture and Industry, Baron Chaptal, in his comprehensive survey *De l'Industrie française* of 1819:

> Machines, which replace the human hand in nearly every operation of manufacturing industry, have worked a great revolution in the arts: since their application, it is no longer possible to calculate products by the number of hands employed since they increase the labour performed ten-fold; and the size of the industry of a country today is measured not by population but by the number of machines.[23]

His argument was that in the face of the English lead in textile manufacture even a prohibitive tariff would be of little use. 'It was therefore either necessary to give up manufacture or imitate their methods.' Chaptal noted that if machine-based manufacture was less extensive in France than in England, this was in part because labour was cheaper in France, but also because the low cost of English fuel made it everywhere advantageous to employ steam engines.[24]

Chaptal also initiated another influential line of interpretation by arguing that the advance of mechanical invention in England was matched by chemical innovation in France.[25] This suggestion was never to be popular among those wishing to link the uniqueness of British industrialisation with the diffusion of practical scientific knowledge across the social structure. Nor was it well received in Britain at the time. According to the *Edinburgh Review*, reviewing Chaptal, the characteristic French invention was the hot air balloon: 'showy, enterprising, holding out to unstaid imaginations, a hope of utility, of which philosophy could easily demonstrate the folly', and, despite its occasional military use, 'now handed over to the Vauxhalls and Ranelaghs, the Tivolis and Folies Beaujours of the day'.[26]

In Say's pamphlet, the machine and the steam engine were treated as partial remedies for an otherwise crushing fiscal burden placed upon British trade by the state. The idea that the new technology might itself constitute a problem was not even considered.

By 1819, however, the problem of unsold goods in the

depressed markets of Europe and North America and of unemployed operatives in the manufacturing districts of Britain had dragged on with greater or lesser intensity for over four years. It was in this situation that the new industrial system itself began to come under direct and sustained attack in Sismondi's *Nouveaux principes d'économie politique ou de la richesse dans ses rapports avec la population.*[27]

Like Say, though on a more modest scale, Sismondi had first made his name as an economist with an exposition of Adam Smith's theory, *De la richesse commerciale, ou principes d'économie politique appliqués à la legislation du commerce*, which had appeared in 1803. But although he protested that Smith's principles continued to serve as a guide, the *Nouveaux principes* could be read as a prolonged account of how the advent of the machine had destroyed Smith's benign picture of the relationship between competition, the division of labour and the extension of the market.[28] Sismondi presented a very different picture of Britain's problems from that provided by Say. Indeed, the denial of what became known as 'Say's Law' – the claim that there could be no general overproduction except as a passing problem resulting from institutional obstacles or imperfect information relating to particular commodities – was one of the central arguments of the book. But Sismondi's intended target was not Say, with whom he had been in friendly correspondence since 1807. Say never became an apologist for the existing state of affairs, in which, he argued, seven-eighths of the population remained without the most rudimentary 'things which the English call "comfortables"'. In the first edition of his *Traité*, Say had himself criticised the domination of unskilled workers by employers and had conceded the need for more state intervention. If Sismondi's attack was directed against any particular 'school' of political economy, it was that of Ricardo, which was attacked for 'making an abstraction of time and space'. Sismondi's expressed aim was to protest against 'the modern organisation of society'. The Ricardian school, it was implied, were its apologists.[29]

Sismondi's critique started out from the commercial crisis which had afflicted Europe since the peace.

> We have seen merchandise of every description, but especially that of England, the great manufacturing power, abounding in all the markets of Italy, in quantities so much in excess of demand, that merchants, in order to save a part of their funds, have been obliged to dispose of them at a quarter or third's loss. The torrent of merchandise pushed out of Italy, has been thrown upon Germany, upon Russia, upon Brazil and has soon encountered the same obstacles there.

And even more extraordinary:

> For the first time the strange phenomenon has been seen of England sending cotton fabrics to India and consequently succeeding at working more cheaply than the half-naked

inhabitants of Hindustan and reducing its workers to an existence yet more miserable.[30]

All this proved that the impossibility of the glutting of markets proclaimed in principle by Say and Ricardo was untrue.[31] Sismondi considered that overproduction had become a property of the economic system once the extent of the market had overreached national boundaries, and that this had been the result of mechanisation. 'Europe has reached the point of possessing in all its parts an industry and a manufacture superior to its needs.'[32] The competition on the world market had intensified because in each country production now surpassed consumption. 'The manufacturers of English stockings before the invention of the framework knitting machine only supplied English consumers; from the time of that invention until it was imitated abroad, its consumers comprised the whole continent.'[33] Each of these industrial inventions, therefore, had killed off other producers 'at great distances', which meant that their suffering went unrecorded while the inventor and the new producers, unaware of their victims, were saluted as benefactors of humanity.[34] Glutted markets and the ruin of rival producers on a world scale were the products of the internationalisation of competition brought about by the machine.

Sismondi deserves recognition, among other things, as a forgotten progenitor of the modern explanation of the population rise from the middle of the eighteenth century.

He had been an early opponent of Malthus's theory of population and, in a book-length entry on 'Political Economy' for Brewster's *Edinburgh Encyclopedia* in 1815, had written a sharp attack. Malthus's principle that 'the population of every country is limited by the quantity of subsistence which that country can furnish' would come true 'only when applied to the whole terrestrial globe, or to a country which has no possibility of trade … Population has never reached the limit of subsistence, and probably it never will. Long before the population can be arrested by the inability of the country to produce more food, it is arrested by the inability of the population to purchase that food, or to labour in producing it.'

Malthus's contrast between geometrical and arithmetical ratios was 'completely sophistical'. 'Abstractly, the multiplication of food follows a geometrical progression, no less than the multiplication of men.' There was a real and serious problem, but Malthus had misdiagnosed it:

> The demand for labour which the capital of a country can pay, and not the quantity of food which that country can produce, regulates the population … Very few men will think of marrying and burdening their hands with the subsistence of individuals unable to procure it themselves, till they have first acquired an establishment. But whenever a new demand for labour raises their wages, and thus increases their revenue, they hasten to satisfy one of the first laws of nature and seek in marriage a

new source of happiness. If the rise of wages was but momentary; if, for example, the favours granted by government suddenly gave a great development to a species of manufacture, which after its commencement, cannot be maintained, the workmen whose remuneration was double during some time will all have married to profit by their opulence; and then, at the moment when their trade declines, families disproportionate to the actual demand of labour, will be plunged into the most dreadful wretchedness.[35]

As Sismondi elaborated his approach in the *Nouveaux principes*, the increase in population was associated with a fall in the age of marriage consequent upon the displacement of peasants and artisans by a swelling class of day-labourers. 'Thus the more the poor man is deprived of all property, the more he is in danger of misjudging his income and of contributing to the growth of a population, which, since it no longer corresponds in any way to demand for labour, will not find subsistence.'[36] In the days when competition had been limited by the guilds, journeymen only married when they became masters and mendicity was contained, a matter only of individual misfortune. Now in England, where a population of day-labourers – condemned never to possess anything – had almost wholly replaced peasants and artisans, begging and pauperism were reaching epidemic proportions, and the shame that formerly accompanied it had disappeared. Furthermore, there was no longer a particular time in a labourer's life at which the choice between marriage and celibacy was best made:

> And as he is accustomed to this uncertainty and as he regards it as the natural situation of the whole of his class, instead of renouncing all pleasures and domestic consolations, he marries as soon as the first good year comes along and wages rise.[37]

The destiny of this class was the same as that whom the Romans called 'proletarians' – 'those who had no property, as if more than all others, were called to have children: *ad prolem generandum*'.[38] In the light of Say's celebration of the independence of the moderns, Sismondi's choice of words was pointed, as were the terms in which he evoked these people. They were a 'miserable and suffering population' which would always be 'restless and a threat to public order'. This was a group of workers 'condemned never to possess anything', 'never to be masters of their fate'. Their masters might dismiss them from one day to the next, because of a bankruptcy or the introduction of a new machine, and this made them dependent on public charity.[39] In England now 10 per cent of the population lived in terrible poverty on public charity. Far from being advantageous, it was contrary to the prosperity of the state to encourage a form of work whose remuneration did not suffice to meet the workers' diverse needs.[40] This unfortunate and dangerous class was a danger to itself and to others:

> It is a misfortune to have called into existence a man
> whom one has at the same time deprived of all pleasures
> which give savour to life, to the country a citizen who has
> no affection for it and no attachment to the established
> order.[41]

The criteria by which Sismondi judged this degrading
condition were not simply humanitarian. They were formed
in particular by two sources: his sense of the prosperity
and gentle social gradations of the Tuscan countryside
– the subject of his first book; and secondly, and more profoundly, his conception of the tradition of the city republic.
Sismondi came from a Protestant Genevan family whose
fortune was mainly lost in investing its funds in Necker's
plan to save the finances of the French state. Forced to leave
Geneva in the revolutionary upheavals, the Sismondi family
settled for five years in the territory of Pescia, near Lucca in
Tuscany. In his book on the agriculture of Tuscany of 1801
he extolled 'the modest *podere*, which is cultivated on a rent
of half the produce by a *mezzaiuolo* [partner] who enjoys
without possessing and does not feel he is poor'. Sismondi
'already asked himself "if an active, numerous, and poor
population was not worth more than a small number of idle
and rich inhabitants?"'.[42] In the years after his early exposition of political economy in 1803 through to 1818, he devoted
himself to the work that made him famous, his *History of
the Medieval Italian Republics*,[43] 'of that labyrinth of equal
and independent states, where he saw displayed more great

characters, more ardent passions, more rare talents, more virtue, courage and true greatness, than in a number of indolent monarchies'.[44]

It is clear that Sismondi's conception of the freedom of the commune, in tune with a larger republican tradition, laid particular weight upon the economic regulation employed by the guilds of the medieval Italian communes to prevent extremes of fortune. The defects of these medieval burghers were that they were jealous of their privileges and unwilling to extend them. Nevertheless, 'they did not compete one with another, they did not undersell, they never lowered wages by competition; and as they had no poor, except the small number which had been made incapable of work by an accident, they supported them themselves ... It was never perceived till the Revolution, that charitable relief created poverty.'[45]

In the *Nouveaux principes*, these themes of a 'happy mediocrity of fortune' and of the alarming disappearance of peasants and artisans who had enjoyed 'an honest ease' recurred again. Sismondi conceded that the guilds could not be restored and their restoration was only demanded by the reactionary defenders of former privileges. Nevertheless, he insistently emphasised the communal republican origins of the guilds,[46] and demanded that a comparable means of limiting competition be discovered.

The cause of the creation of the proletarians was above all the machine, which had concentrated production in the hands of a small group of rich merchants while ruining the smaller merchants and manufacturers.[47] As a result of these developments, the interests of manufacturers and that of society no longer coincided.[48] Competition benefited the employer, but he did not have to count its costs:

> Today, a manufacturer, having summoned to himself numerous families, abandons them suddenly without employment, because he has discovered that a steam engine can perform all their work; but he would learn that the steam engine produced no saving, if all the men who were working, found no further means of employment, and if he were obliged to maintain them in the poor house while he heated up his boilers.[49]

As it was, society was left to deal, through public charity or the parish relief, with sickness, old age or unemployment of this dependent workforce.

For Sismondi, the problems of England were not those of a corrupt militarist state relying on colonialism and protection, but of a state guided by economists constantly repeating, '*Laissez faire et laissez passer.*'[50] The example of England had seduced the statesmen of Europe. But in reality it was a terrible warning of the danger of 'resting the whole of political economy upon the principle of competition without limits'. It was the place where the interest of humanity had been sacrificed to the sum of individual cupidities and as a result was 'the only nation' which 'sees constantly contrasted its apparent wealth with the terrifying poverty of a tenth of its population reduced to dependence on public relief'.[51] Sismondi hoped that if his warnings were too late to change the direction taken by England, it might at least be of use to humanity and his compatriots in avoiding the path of unlimited competition elsewhere.

Sismondi's work was barely noticed in England, where his critical writings on political economy were not even translated in fragmentary form until 1847.[52] But they made considerable impact in France and the rest of western Europe, where his critique was selectively appropriated in socialist, legitimist and even liberal economic criticism.[53] More specifically, it was in response to Sismondi that the notion of an 'industrial revolution' surfaced in France in the 1820s in the writings of Say.

The disagreements which the post-war commercial depression provoked among political economists surfaced not only in the *Nouveaux principes*, but also in Malthus's *Principles of Political Economy Considered with a View to Their Practical Application*, which appeared in 1820 and raised similar doubts about the impossibility of overproduction. In his response to Malthus in 1821, *Letters to T. R. Malthus on Political Economy and Stagnation of Commerce*, Say also took the opportunity to respond more cursorily to Sismondi. 'There are too many English goods offered in Italy and elsewhere, because there are not a sufficient quantity of Italian goods suited to England.'[54] His political conception of England's problems remained the same: 'I know that certain corrupt and corrupting governments stand in need of monopolies, and customs duties, to pay for the vote of the honourable majorities who pretend to be the representatives of nations.'[55] It was this need which was responsible for the institutional obstacles to the international exchange of goods.

> The English government rejects, on its part, by means of its Customs Houses and importation Duties, the production which the English might bring from abroad, in exchange for their goods, and even the NECESSARY *provisions*, of which their manufactures stand so much in need; and this is because it is necessary that the English farmers should sell their wheat at above eighty shillings per quarter in order to enable them to pay the enormous taxes.[56]

Say did not bother to respond to Sismondi's idea that Europe possessed an industry superior to its wants. He may have considered such arguments had been adequately refuted in the English periodical press. But Sismondi's arguments received more attention in the annual course of lectures which he delivered at the Conservatoire des Arts et Métiers; and the appearance of a second, expanded edition of Sismondi's *Nouveaux principes* in 1827 was answered by an extensive examination of the relationship between employment and the use of machinery in his *Cours complet d'économie politique pratique*, finally published in six volumes in 1828.[57]

Like Sismondi, Say followed Smith in considering changes in the art of manufacture as the result of an extension of the market and consequent sophistication of the division of labour. Hence the importance of improvements in transport. The industry and population of Manchester had tripled since that town had been linked to the port of Liverpool by the Bridgewater canal.[58] Later on, he attacked Sismondi's idea that machines were only a benefit to society when developed to meet an existing need. This, in Say's view, was to assume that needs constituted a fixed quantity, but in reality they were continually redefined as production advanced.[59] Similarly, Say attacked Sismondi's rhetorical declaration for a population of citizens above that of steam engines. Steam engines neither diminished the quantity of products nor the numbers of citizens; they simply encouraged citizens to provide themselves with things which the most civilised peoples generally consumed by means of their capital and industry.[60] It was true that these changing needs might mean that people would be obliged to change their occupations – and this of course was a source of inconvenience – but should these passing but necessary inconveniences arrest the progress by means of which nations had progressed from a state of barbarism to prosperity, civilisation and abundance? Suppose a means had been found to prevent the introduction of cotton-spinning machinery into France, the only result would have been an enormous disparity between domestic and international prices which would have resulted in smuggling and a poverty-stricken, underemployed domestic workforce.

> It is therefore not in order to decide between the use or
> prohibition of machines that it is useful to clarify these
> questions: if one is reasonable, one does not decide
> whether or not to push back a river to its source; but it
> is indeed necessary to foresee the ravages of this river, to
> direct its meanderings, but especially to derive benefits
> from its water.[61]

In fact, Say considered, several factors were likely to lessen
the temporary misfortunes experienced by the working
class as a result of the introduction of machinery. Firstly,
investment in steam engines was expensive. It could only
be undertaken by those possessing considerable capital and
was therefore only likely to be introduced gradually and after
much deliberation. Secondly, while the least skilled opera-
tions might easily be taken over by machines, the process of
mechanisation was likely to become more difficult when it
became a question of replacing more complex activities.[62]

Say then went on to deny that machines were responsible
for the aggregation in manufacturing towns of a working
population which at times either lacked work or was too
poorly paid to subsist. Machinery was not the cause of this
problem. 'There were scarcely any machines in England at
the time of Queen Elizabeth and yet it was then that it was
felt necessary to bring in that law for the support of the
poor, which has only served to multiply them.'[63] In places
where manufacturing industry was most developed, oscillations in employment did not derive from machines but

from the nature of the articles manufactured, which were in general exposed to large vicissitudes in demand. If anything, more mechanised industries were likely to experience more regular employment because of their higher overheads.[64] It was in countries like Poland, where no machinery had been introduced, that the working classes had most reason to complain; or China, where all work was done by hand and people died of starvation.

Say reserved what he considered his strongest point to last: not only does mechanisation reduce costs of production and therefore brings the product within reach of a greater number of consumers, but history has shown that the increase in the number of consumers far exceeds the decrease in price. A memorable historical example of this process was the replacement of the manuscript by the printed book. Not only had the printing press not abridged employment, it had created a vast industry where none had existed before.[65] But, Say continued, 'perhaps the most striking experience, offered by the annals of industry, is provided by the impact made by the machine used in the manufacture of cotton'.[66] Say proposed to devote a whole chapter of the *Cours* to this topic. It would do more than provide an example, it would suggest additional reflections 'on the revolutions of industry and the economy of nations' ['*sur les revolutions de l'industrie et l'économie des nations*'].[67]

In the following chapter, 'on the revolution that has occurred in commerce occasioned by cotton-spinning machinery' ('*De la revolution survenue dans le commerce à l'occasion des machines à filer le coton*'), after surveying the ancient and early modern trade in cotton and after briefly referring to the innovations of Hargreaves and Crompton, Say went on to detail the invention of Arkwright. As a result of Arkwright's discovery and subsequent improvements, a commercial revolution had occurred:

> At the end of the eighteenth century there was not consumed in Europe a single piece of calico which did not reach us from Hindustan; only twenty-five years have passed and not a single piece of calico is consumed, which comes from the country from where they all used to come. Furthermore, English merchants begin successfully to export it to the Indies. It is truly a river which flows back to its source.[68]

Say went on to point out that this revolution, which had been as important as the opening of the trade route to Asia around the Cape of Good Hope, had enormously increased the numbers of workers employed in the industry and raised their wages. So far as there was evidence of recent wage cuts in England, Say attributed it to a wave of Irish immigration.[69] Even in the case of India, Say claimed that there was no evidence to suggest that the condition of Indian manufacturers had become worse than before. This was because calico production in India could still count on an enormous domestic market.[70] Furthermore, while the export of calicos had diminished, this had been more than compensated by a much greater rise in the export of indigo, sugar and cotton wool. Indeed, as a result of the invention of machinery, there had been a substantial increase in the production of cotton all over the world. Finally, the impact made by cotton-spinning machinery was not confined to the textile industry. The great increase in the production of cotton goods stimulated the production of other goods, with which cotton goods could be exchanged. 'It is in this way that a single industry can extend its influence over the whole economy of nations.'[71]

In Say's work dating back to the beginning of the French Revolution, *industrie* – aboriginally the quality associated by Franklin and Price with a virtuous life in the simple commonwealths of North America – had been presented as the answer to poverty. Poverty had been linked with dependence, either with the feudal and clerical residues of force and fraud or with the militarism and clientelism of the ancients revived in the wars of Napoleon. In Say's *Cours complet*, which appeared at the end of the 1820s, the association between *industrie* and the 'independence' of the moderns had been extended to include the astonishing '*revolutions d'industrie*' which were now transforming the poverty and backwardness of Europe and the wider world. *Industrie* and its revolutions were not, therefore, as Donald Coleman argued, a child of romanticism, but the unanticipated enlargement of what had originally been designed as the binding ethos of a modern republic.[72] But from the 1830s even liberals and republicans became uncomfortably aware that industriousness and frugality – homespun and useful enough formulae in eighteenth-century small town Pennsylvania – connected only remotely with the commercial volatility of modern industry. Furthermore, the exclusion or disfranchisement of the majority of the wage-earning classes – henceforth 'the working classes' or 'working class' – transformed advice on industry and thrift, as part of the ethos of an all-inclusive republic, into the hypocritical sermonising of a triumphant and self-satisfied 'bourgeoisie'.

V

THE WEALTH OF MIDAS

Say's '*revolutions d'industrie*' were the principal source of the account of the English 'industrial revolution' given by Jérome Adolphe Blanqui (the brother of the famous French revolutionary Auguste Blanqui) in his *Histoire de l'économie politique* of 1837.[1] Blanqui was a protégé of Say who had gained him the chair of history and industrial economy at the École Spéciale du Commerce.[2] Blanqui also gave courses at the Athenée and at the Conservatoire des Arts et Métiers, where in 1833 he succeeded Say as professor. Following Say, Blanqui wrote of the impact of the Bridgewater canal and emphasised how cotton-spinning machinery and the steam engine had overturned the old system of commerce. He repeated Say's point about the reversal of the movement of cotton goods between Europe and Hindustan, which he similarly compared to a river flowing backwards to its source.[3]

But Blanqui was not an uncritical follower of Say. He considered Say too close to 'the English school' which paid undue attention to production at the expense of producers.[4]

He admired the fact that Say related economics to practice in contrast to 'the abstractions' of Ricardo, but thought him too harsh towards the state and too indulgent towards capital.[5] 'He was seduced by the wonders of English industry, modern manufacturing industry, and did not have the time to appreciate all the afflictions that followed in its wake ... He attributed the wound of pauperism in that country to purely political causes. The glutting of markets seemed to him to be solely the consequence of commercial restrictions.' What was lacking in Say was a viewpoint that was more 'social' and more 'elevated' on questions of pauperism and wages.[6]

In contrast to the 'English school', which only regarded the production of wealth as 'an element of national power', France's privilege was 'to defend the rights of humanity'.[7] Thus while English industry advanced with giant steps, French writers recalled the 'sacred principles' of the equitable division of the profits of labour. Blanqui considered himself to belong to 'the social era' of political economy.[8]

What this meant, above all, was taking seriously the contrast between conspicuous opulence and extreme poverty in England, as highlighted by Sismondi. But Blanqui's stance in relation to Sismondi's critique was ultimately not so dissimilar from that of Say. If the progress of manufactures, the improvement of machines or the multiplication of the means of production by the banks had really been the scourges that Sismondi claimed, how could one explain a growth of national prosperity which had affected even the humblest workers?[9] This surely proved that all economies in the cost of production were gains made by the whole of society, even if in a very uneven manner. Like Malthus, Sismondi had been diverted by his obsession with one simple idea, and he had confused the functioning of the system with its abuses. Nevertheless, as Blanqui willingly conceded:

The opinions of M. de Sismondi have exerted a great influence in Europe. It is he who has been the first to reveal the secret of these social misfortunes, mainly concentrated in manufacturing countries, and who has sounded the alarm about the danger of the banks, well before the recent catastrophes which have so sadly confirmed his predictions. Thanks to him, the condition of the worker has become something sacred and precious; he has had his place at the banquet of life, from which the theories of Malthus wished to exclude him; and henceforth the progress of wealth will not be considered as truly useful, except to the extent that its benefits will spread out to include all those who will take part. The principle has been posed, it is for systems of legislation to draw out the consequences.[10]

According to Blanqui, the evils of industrial society included the universality of competition, the continued abuse of political privileges, the struggle of large and small capitals and the unequal distribution of taxation. His account of the English 'industrial revolution' therefore contained a social dimension largely absent from Say. Blanqui claimed that the invention of machinery had not only transformed commerce, but had also produced the conditions in which small producers were becoming the tributaries of large capitalists. The emancipation of labour had not occurred either in France or Britain. In France, the promise of emancipation which followed the suppression of the guilds had been contradicted by continued commercial protection which preserved the privileges of certain groups and resulted in 'a true commercial feudalism'. In England, 'patriarchal labour' had been transformed into 'industrial feudalism' in which the worker became anew 'the serf' of the workshop tied to 'the glebe of wages'.[11]

England had sacrificed all social considerations to the creation of wealth and thus, while the English had developed the productive powers of the nation beyond measure, they had not devoted proportionate care to the well-being of the workers. This was not a socialist argument, but a radical–liberal criticism in line with Say. 'The all-powerful aristocracy in England finds it simple to impose upon labour all the burdens of taxation',[12] and it was taxation, as Say had argued in his pamphlet on the English, which had pushed England on to its singular industrial path. Blanqui repeated the theme. 'The continual increase of taxes, mainly on articles of consumption, has condemned the inhabitants of this country to a continual fever of improvement. England has become an immense factory, a universal emporium.'[13]

Blanqui wrote after the 1830 revolution in France during

the period of the July Monarchy. These years, in which government once more identified itself with the moderate gains of the original Revolution, witnessed the return – though in milder form – of some of the tensions of Thermidor. The regime was opposed by republicans, Jacobins and communists on the left, and by legitimists and Catholics on the right. Louis Philippe was 'the citizen king', in many ways the embodiment of what the Abbé Sieyès had hoped from a republican monarchy in the 1790s; and the franchise was restricted, much as it had been in 1795. Similarly, an Académie des Sciences Morales et Politiques was founded in order to resume the work of the Institut, which had been so abruptly closed down by Napoleon. Backed by government support and confident that scientific investigation would find a means of resolving what contemporaries had begun to call 'the social problem', the academy encouraged leading academicians like Blanqui and the social statistician Villermé to examine the phenomenon of pauperism.

Villermé's enquiry into the condition of workers in the textile industry became famous when its results were published in a two-volume study in 1840, *Tableau de l'état physique et moral des ouvriers employés dans les manufactures de coton, de laine et de soie*. His general conclusions were optimistic in the tradition of Say. He argued that 'industry' had improved the condition of the worker. The people were better dressed and better fed. The bread eaten by the poor was better than it had formerly been, white bread had ceased to be a luxury and in the towns the same bread was eaten by rich and poor.

But what caught the attention of contemporaries were not the bland conclusions of the report but its detailed descriptions, which were unexpected and disturbing. As one of his strongest critics, the Catholic social observer Eugène Buret pointed out, Villermé's account of the condition of the textile workers themselves did not correspond at all comfortably with these generalisations. Villermé revealed that only with great difficulty did wages cover the basic needs of households and that employment, like health, remained chronically uncertain. The working day in the textile factories was also inhumanly long, varying from fifteen to seventeen hours, with only one and a half hours allowed for meals. Most shocking especially to those who had placed so much emphasis upon a change of manners of the people, were the revelations about morals in the towns. Particularly striking was the observation that in large towns the choice for workers was not between marriage and celibacy, but between marriage and 'concubinage', since the practice of cohabitation was pervasive.

Villermé, for all his general belief in improvement, offered a sober corrective to Say's emphasis upon 'frugality'. He noted that while the number of savings banks had increased, they remained virtually unknown in the countryside, and that in the towns they were mainly used by domestic servants and other single persons, rather than by manual workers. Workers, especially those with families, tended to join friendly societies as a form of insurance against sickness. But the rate of failure of these societies was high, since they were generally run by people without knowledge of the actuarial principles necessary to keep them afloat. Villermé believed that while 'industriousness' and 'frugality' described the habits of only a minority of workers, change would depend upon 'the education and moralisation of workers'.[14] But others pointed to a more concrete and immediate difficulty: uncertainty and volatility of employment. As Buret put it, 'a caprice, a rumour on the stock exchange, some distant event happening at the other end of the world can put machines out of action and with them thousands of hands'.[15]

The difficulty was no longer simply economic or moral, it had become political. The government no longer confronted the poor, but the 'working classes', or as Sismondi had described them, 'the proletariat'. According to Adolphe Blanqui, two battles were yet to be won. The first was the continuing addiction of governments to protection, the second the emancipation of the workers:

> [T]he battlefield is no longer on the plains, but in the workshops … This is a true war, where the combatants employ ingenious and powerful machines which on the terrain of pauperism leave millions of workers gasping for breath, men and women, without concern for old age or infancy. It is a serious conflict between different classes of workers … France appears to oppose England, but capital struggles far more deeply against the worker.[16]

The causes of the weakness of Louis Philippe's 'July Monarchy', which lasted from 1830 until its downfall in the revolution of 1848, and the reasons why it gave birth to the struggle between the 'bourgeois' and 'the proletarians' were clearly perceived by a Prussian observer, Lorenz von Stein. Writing in 1842, Stein argued that the preconditions for the appearance of a proletariat had been laid by the French Revolution, for there could be no proletariat so long as birth rather than property was the precondition of participation within the state. In 1814, despite the restoration of the monarchy, a property qualification remained a condition for political participation, thus allying monarchy to property and alienating the people.

But the contradiction became more glaring in July 1830, when all prerogatives of birth were abolished. This left property as the only qualification for participation in political life, just at a time when the extension of the division of labour described by Adam Smith made it increasingly difficult for a person to acquire independence and property by means of his labour. The result was a swelling, propertyless class whose social struggles could not but challenge the existence of the state.

> The class of the property-less has become a single whole; it has acquired a consciousness of its condition; it recognises that this condition is based upon laws which go beyond individuals; it feels itself to be governed by a power with which it has struggled uselessly; it is excluded from real

participation in the power of the state; it understands the impossibility of the great mass of its members being able to climb out of it into a higher class; it has thus become an estate, and this estate – at the same time the embodiment of all the demands which the principle of equality has raised without being able to satisfy – is the French proletariat.[17]

Henceforth, as all appeared to agree, an end to poverty had become inseparable from the emancipation of labour.

❧

Blanqui's 'industrial revolution' took place in Britain. He confidently ascribed its beginnings to the inventions of Watt and Arkwright.[18] But any question about the effect of industrialisation upon ideas about the end of poverty ran up against an intriguing prior puzzle: that, despite ubiquitous contact between the two countries, in Britain the notion of an 'industrial revolution' was not employed. When the political economist J. R. McCulloch discussed the large changes which had occurred in Britain in the decades before 1850, he reflected that

> extraordinary changes occasioned by the late war in every department of the public economy deeply affected the interests of all classes, and created the most anxious and universal attention. The experience of centuries was crowded into the short space of thirty years; and while

> novel combinations of circumstances served as tests by
> which to try existing theories, they enabled even inferior
> writers to extend the boundaries of the science and to
> become the discoverers of new truths.[19]

The changes that McCulloch went on to specify were
the suspension of cash payments by the Bank of England,
the battle over the Corn Laws and the emergence of new
general theories of rent and distribution. But they did not
include the 'industrial revolution'. Similarly, neither Harriet
Martineau in her *History of England during the Thirty Years'
Peace*, published in 1849, nor G. R. Porter in his *Progress
of the Nation* of 1847, employed the notion of an 'industrial revolution' as either a phrase or as a concept. Since it is
likely that these writers were conversant with French debate,
this omission suggests that important political issues were
at stake in the choice of language in discussing economic
change in Britain. For, quite clearly, they were aware of the
magnitude of the industrial change taking place around
them.

McCulloch, describing the development of cotton manufacture in the *Edinburgh Review* in 1827, wrote: '[T]he
rapid growth and prodigious magnitude of the cotton
manufacture of Great Britain, are beyond all question the
most extraordinary phenomena in the history of industry.'[20]
Just like Say, he wondered that 'neither the extreme cheap-
ness of labour in Hindustan, nor the perfection to which
the natives had previously attained, has enabled them to

withstand the competition of those who buy their cotton, and who after carrying it five thousand miles to be manufactured, carry back the goods to them. This is the greatest triumph of mechanical genius.'[21]

In Martineau's case, it was rather as if by mid-century she had become weary of reiterating once more an oft-repeated point:

> Of steam and railways enough has been said. Everybody knows more than could be told here of what they do in superseding toil, in setting human hands free for skilled labour, in bringing men face to face with each other and with nature and novelty.[22]

Porter similarly wrote of the rise of cotton manufacture in Britain as 'perhaps the most extraordinary page in the annals of human industry'.[23] Thus, by the 1840s, although the term 'industrial revolution' was not employed, the belief that what had occurred in industry belonged to the realms of the extraordinary had become a commonplace.

Unsurprisingly, political economists were monitoring changes in the economy quite closely and their changing preoccupations from the 1810s to the 1840s were broadly in accord with the chronology of the 'industrial revolution' now offered by economic historians. Before the 1830s, dramatic increases in productivity were associated with a few exceptional industries.[24] Citations from Baines, Ure, Gaskell, Porter and others, often used as the basis of later general statements about the 'industrial revolution', were in fact mainly depictions of the new technology of the textile industry.[25] These technological advances were not generally considered in macroeconomic terms, but treated as part of a quite extraordinary transformation of production which had occurred in one or two sectors or regions. The overall analytical framework within which assumptions about economic development were made was, until the 1830s, based on Smith's model of the division of labour. But thereafter Nassau Senior began to argue that there was no reason why 'the improvements of the next sixty years should not equal those of the preceding', that 'the cotton machinery ... receives daily improvements', and that 'the steam engine is in its infancy'.[26]

Similarly, on the question of machinery, the original Smithian view that every increase in capital set in motion an additional quantity of labour was already questioned in 1817, when John Barton pointed out that this held true only in the case of circulating capital, not of fixed capital. The acceptance of this criticism by England's greatest economist at the time, David Ricardo, in the third edition of his *Principles* caused some consternation among his followers, but by and large remained marginal to the debates and assumptions of political economists in the 1820s.[27] By the 1830s, however, it appears that economists were beginning to distance themselves from the Malthusian theory of population, the Ricardian theory of rent and the Smithian picture of labour.[28] They began more serious and extensive investigations into the economic role of machinery, fixed capital and inanimate power. At the same time, what might be thought of as the first generation of management consultants began to publish detailed examinations of the labour process in the factory. The most famous of these new experts was Andrew Ure, who referred to the change which had occurred as a 'revolution':

> When the first water-frames for spinning cotton were erected at Cromford, in the romantic valley of the Derwent, about sixty years ago, mankind were little aware of the mighty revolution which the new system of labour was destined to achieve, not only in the structure of British society, but in the fortunes of the world at large. Arkwright alone had the sagacity to discern, and the boldness to predict in glowing language, how vastly productive human industry would become, when no longer proportioned in its results to muscular effort, which is by its nature fitful and capricious, but when made to consist in the task of guiding the work of mechanical fingers and arms, regularly impelled with great velocity by some indefatigable physical power.[29]

Indeed, Ure went further and highlighted the fundamental change, which he thought had occurred in the principle of the division of labour since the time of Adam Smith and, in so doing, provided the basis of Marx's depiction of modern industry in *Capital*:

When Adam Smith wrote his immortal elements of economics, automatic machinery being hardly known, he was properly led to regard the division of labour as the grand principle of manufacturing improvement; and he showed in the example of pin-making, how each handicraftsman, being thereby enabled to perfect himself by practice in one point, became a quicker and cheaper workman ... But what was in Dr Smith's time a topic of useful illustration, cannot now be used without risk of misleading the public mind as to the right principle of manufacturing industry. In fact, the division, or rather adaptation of labour to the different talents of men, is little thought of in factory employment. On the contrary, wherever a process requires peculiar dexterity and steadiness of hand, it is withdrawn as soon as possible from the *cunning* workman, who is prone to irregularities of many kinds, and it is placed in the hands of a peculiar mechanism, so self-regulating that a child may superintend it.[30]

It was still later – towards the end of the 1840s when, according to Von Tunzelmann's and Wrigley's chronology, steam had become a major source of energy across the economy as a whole – that the implications of a regular and manageable source of inanimate power was distinguished from the gains associated with machinery.[31] In Senior's lectures of 1847, the attributes of both machinery and labour were now derived from the domination of a moving power.[32] Economists were not remote from the development of industrial Britain. In the 1830s and 1840s they attempted to consider the significance of the factory, mechanised production and steam power, just as in the 1810s and 1820s they had debated the problems of rising population and differential rent.

In the case of the predominant language of government from the 1810s to the 1840s, that of 'liberal Toryism', the reasons for resisting notions of an industrial revolution, as with the associated ideas on the emancipation of labour found in the works of Say and Blanqui, were clearly political and religious rather than economic. According to Boyd Hilton, there were 'two discrete, if sometime overlapping models of Free Trade' in the first half of the nineteenth century.

The first, and more familiar, of these was that of professional economists like Ricardo: 'expansionist, industrialist, competitive, and cosmopolitan'. But there was a second, 'more widespread and probably more influential', especially upon liberal Tory administrations between Liverpool and Peel: that of the Evangelicals, voiced by Malthus disciple Thomas Chalmers. This alternative version of free trade was 'static (or cyclical), nationalist, retributive, and purgative, employing competition as a means to education rather than to growth'.[33] Its followers' preoccupation was not the elimination of poverty, but the economy as a system of natural justice. They believed that the health of the economy and polity was dependent upon the observance of a moral code. The punitive implications of Malthus's theodicy were developed in emphatically Christian terms. The market was sanctified as an impersonal agent of moral law. It not only allocated resources, but rewarded virtue and punished vice. The task of the legislator was therefore to remove 'artificial' constraints on the operation of the market in order that morality should prevail.

Evangelical understandings of the economy in the pre-1850 period were in no sense incompatible with a vivid appreciation of the changes brought about by scientific and industrial innovation. On the contrary, the magnitude of these changes was fully acknowledged. What distinguished evangelical liberal Toryism from other, more secular forms of discourse was the meaning it attached to such changes – national and religious, providential or apocalyptic, the saving of England in the darkest hour of its battle against atheist France. A striking example is provided by the address given by the then-president of the Board of Trade William Huskisson in 1824, in the presence of Lord Liverpool, to a public meeting called to erect a monument to James Watt. He began by talking about the moral and Christian benefits conferred by steam:

> In my view of the subject, there is no portion of the globe, however remote where the name and flag of England are known, where commerce has carried her sails and begun to introduce the arts of civilisation which does not derive some advantage from Mr Watt's discoveries. The economy and abridgement of labour, the perfection and rapidity of

manufacture, the cheap and almost indefinite multiplication of every article which suits the luxury, the convenience, or the wants of mankind are all so many means of creating, in men even but little advanced from the savage state, a taste for improvement … If the steam engine be the most powerful instrument in the hands of man, to alter the face of the physical world, it operates, at the same time, as a powerful moral lever in forwarding the great cause of civilisation.[34]

Within Huskisson's evangelical cosmology there was no dissonance between these universal Christian benefits bestowed by steam and the salvation of the nation by steam in its hour of peril.

Looking back … to the demands which were made upon the resources of this country during the late war, perhaps it is not too much to say, at least it is my opinion, that those resources might have failed us, before that war was brought to a safe and glorious conclusion, but for the creations of Mr Watt, and of others moving in the same career, by whose discoveries those resources were so greatly multiplied and increased. It is perhaps not too much to say, that, but for the vast accession thus imperceptibly made to the general wealth of this empire, we might have been driven to sue for peace, before, the march and progress of events, Nelson had put forth the last energies of his naval genius at Trafalgar, or, at any rate

179

before Wellington had put the final seal to the security of
Europe at Waterloo.[35]

Steam as an engine of war which secured British victory
in the Napoleonic wars became something of a commonplace. According to Porter, writing over twenty years
later, 'but for the invention of the spinning jenny and the
improvements in the steam engine, which have produced
such almost magical effects upon the productive energies of
this kingdom, it would have been impossible to have with-
stood the combination with which, single-handed, we were
called upon to contend'.[36] It led French commentators like
Blanqui to believe that lack of reference to an 'industrial
revolution' and to its social dimension was to be attributed
to an exclusive preoccupation of 'the English school' with
national power or production rather than producers.[37]

Such a belief, often reiterated by continental socialists,
dated back to the generally hostile French reaction to Ricardo,
whom Sismondi accused of being abstract and deduc-
tive, and others considered lacking in human concern.[38]
The fact that Ricardo changed his position on machinery
appears to have gone unnoticed, and nor do such accusations apply at all accurately to other members of the Ricardian school. J. R. McCulloch, one of the most prolific writers
on political economy in the period, was often regarded
as a dogmatic populariser of Ricardo. He was accused by
Blanqui of having adopted 'the inflexible absolutism of the
manufacturing system which consists in advancing produc-

tion without consideration for the producer, if not through indifference for humanity, at least by abuse of principles'.[39] Yet McCulloch remained firmly in favour of the regulation of child labour and his view of the factory system can hardly be described as panglossian. Writing about the manufacturing system in 1845, he stated:

> It is impossible at this moment to cast the horoscope of this system, to foresee its revolutions, or to estimate its future influence over society. We confess, however, that our anticipations are not of the most agreeable kind. It appears to be, of its essence, that most sorts of employments should be conducted on a large and continually increasing scale, in great establishments, with the assistance of highly improved and expensive machinery; providing, in this way, for the exaltation of a few individuals by the irremediable helotism of the great majority. And this conclusion would seem to be consistent not only with the nature of manufacturing industry, but with the fact that, though there has been a vast increase of production, and of wealth and comforts among the upper classes engaged in business during the last twenty or thirty years, and a considerable diminution of taxation, the condition of the workpeople during that period has rather, we incline to think, been sensibly deteriorated.[40]

Harriet Martineau, another famous populariser and author of the fictional series *Illustrations of Political*

Economy, was also tentative. In her monumental *History of England During the Thirty Years' Peace*, which appeared in 1849–50, after endeavouring to sum up all the progressive changes which had occurred during the period, she asked what remained to be done. Her conclusion was not unlike that of the French:

> The tremendous Labour Question remains absolutely untouched – the question whether the toil of life is not to provide a sufficiency of bread. No thoughtful man can for a moment suppose that this question can be put aside. No man with a head and a heart can suppose that any considerable class of a nation will submit for ever to toil incessantly for bare necessaries – without comfort, ease, or luxury, now – without a prospect for their children, and without a hope for their own old age. A social idea or system which compels such a state of things as this must be, is in so far, worn out.[41]

The real reason why liberal and radical political economists in the first half of the nineteenth century were reluctant to adopt the language of *industrie* and of the 'industrial revolution' was because, in the context of British politics, this language was suspected of providing a wilful and sometimes sinister distraction from the real cause of poverty, misery and corruption: the warlike, protectionist and debt-ridden aristocratic state. This was clear, to begin with, in the liberal and radical reaction to Robert Owen's proposals to cure post-war distress. It was Owen who, around 1819, more than any other writer in Britain, spoke of industrial and social change in terms nearest to an idea of 'industrial revolution'. In the years after the battle of Waterloo, he was the first to refer in apocalyptic terms to the changes which had occurred in manufacture and trade as a result of the introduction of cotton-spinning machinery and the steam engine during the wars. He talked about the arrival of 'a crisis, new in the history of mankind'.[42] 'The immediate effects of this manufacturing phenomenon were a rapid increase of the wealth, industry, population, and political influence of the British Empire.' But, he went on, 'the general diffusion of manufactures throughout a country generates a new character in its inhabitants; and as this character is formed upon a principle quite unfavourable to individual or general happiness, it will produce the most lamentable and permanent evils unless its tendency be counteracted by legislative interference and direction'.[43]

Owen proclaimed his dislike of 'class, sect and party' and his distance from politics. Radicals and liberals understandably distrusted his proposals for the relief of post-war unemployment and his 'villages of industry'. 'Must the whole world be converted into a cotton factory?' Hazlitt complained. 'Our statesmen are not afraid of the perfect system of reform he talks of, and, in the meantime, his cant against reform in Parliament, and about Bonaparte, serves as a practical diversion in their favour.'[44] His admirers included members of the royal house, like Queen

Victoria's father, the Duke of Kent, and high Tories like Sidmouth.

It was not, therefore, simply Owen's incompetence as a political economist that explained the savage review given to his proposals by Robert Torrens in the *Edinburgh Review* in October 1819.[45] Torrens' diagnosis of the economic problems of post-war Britain was expressed in Ricardian terms. He conceded that the transition from war to peace might for a time have disturbed due proportion in the quantities of the different articles brought to market. But the more serious and lasting causes of depression were agricultural protection which resulted in the enforced cultivation of inferior lands, other 'barbarous restrictions on commerce' which by preventing exchanges hampered the export of manufactures, and taxation which appropriated a large proportion of the surplus of industry. Should 'fettered trade' and 'oppressive taxes' continue, Torrens considered, 'England, like Holland, must gradually cease to be a manufacturing and commercial, and consequently a rich and powerful country'.[46] In these circumstances, far from being a source of problems, by cutting production costs the steam engine made possible a continuing export trade which protectionist Britain would otherwise have lost. 'The steam engine has fought our battles and pays the interest of our debt. If our improved machinery did not tend to reduce the expenses of producing manufactured goods, we could neither sell our fabrics in the foreign market, nor keep our inferior lands under cultivation.'[47]

According to Torrens, Owen was 'profoundly ignorant of all the laws which regulate the production and distribution of wealth'. He 'tells us that the distress to which the people of this country are exposed arises from scientific and mechanical power producing more than the existing regulation of society permit to be consumed. This is tantamount to saying that wealth is poverty, and that the necessaries of life are unobtainable, because they exist in excess.'[48] Furthermore, Owen's proposals were ambiguous. They had not specified whether these 'villages of cooperation', which combined industry with 'spade husbandry', were to be autarkic or whether they were to engage in exchange. For Torrens, this meant one of two possibilities:

> If Mr Owen retain the division of labour in his establishments, the changes in the state of external markets, and the consequent impossibility of obtaining an uniformly profitable sale for their productions will occasionally deprive his villagers of the means of paying their rent and taxes, and reduce them to the condition of bankrupts and paupers; and, if, to avoid such evils, he discard the divisions of labour, and cause each establishment to consume within itself whatever it supplies, then the great principle which multiplies the effective powers of industry will be thrown out of operation, all the sources of prosperity will be dried up, and universal poverty overspread the land.[49]

It was no doubt the fact that Sismondi's *Nouveaux*

principes was associated in the minds of political economists with Owen's proposal, which explains why his work made such little impact in Britain. Sismondi had met Owen in Paris in the years after Waterloo. Later, in the second edition of *Nouveaux principes*, he stated that, although he disagreed with Owen's cooperative remedies, he shared Owen's claim that production with the aid of steam and machinery created overproduction.[50] It was, therefore, not surprising that Torrens should have appended to his attack upon Owen an additional refutation of Sismondi in defence of the principle that 'the power of consuming necessarily increases with every increase in the power of producing'. The point was made even more trenchantly in 1821 by a reviewer of 'The Opinions of Messrs. Say, Sismondi and Malthus on the Effects of Machinery and Accumulation, Stated and Examined':

> [L]et us not, therefore, attempt to excuse the drivelling incapacity of our statesmen, by ascribing the difficulties which are the necessary consequences of their blind and perverse policy, to the admirable innovations of our engineers, and the skill and industry of our artisans. But let us acknowledge, that, had it not been for these innovations, all the difficulties in which we are at present involved, would have been aggravated in a tenfold proportion.[51]

In France, after the July revolution of 1830, an Orleanist 'social' liberal like Blanqui could accept that the questions raised by Sismondi about the condition of the industrial worker deserved serious attention. Now that aristocracy and church no longer ruled, it was possible to make a reality of the emancipation of labour promised by the French Revolution. Rational enquiry, such as that conducted by Villermé, culminating in judiciously formulated legislation would produce a solution to the labour question. In this respect, Blanqui was only expressing the early hopes of the July Monarchy which, as Maurice Agulhon has pointed out, was exceptional in its encouragement of serious and disinterested social research.[52] Britain, by contrast, remained a state dominated and to a large extent governed by a powerful aristocracy, both before and after 1832. The criticisms voiced by Owen, Sismondi or Southey remained unacceptable to the majority of liberals and radicals because that would mean an abandonment of their starting point, the attack on a state based on force and fraud with its attendant evils of clientelism, misgovernment, militarism, unequal taxation, colonialism and commercial protection.

In the period after Waterloo there had been considerable overlap in the opinions of the heirs to 'the party of philosophy' in France and in Britain the grouping who became known as the 'philosophical radicals' – the young intellectuals, journalists and would-be politicians who clustered around Jeremy Bentham and James Mill. For this group in the 1820s, political economy and the view that human character was formed by 'circumstances', i.e. environment, were as important as the particular opinions of

Bentham. According to the recollections of John Stuart Mill, 'So complete was my father's reliance on the influence of reason over the minds of mankind, wherever it is allowed to reach them that he felt as if all would be gained if the whole population were taught to read.' He believed that 'when the legislature no longer represented a class interest, it would aim at the general interest, honestly and with adequate wisdom'. Furthermore, 'next to the aristocracy, an established church, or corporation of priests, as being by position the great depravers of mankind, and interested in opposing the progress of the human mind, was the object of his greatest detestation'. The most formative book of John Stuart Mill's boyhood was Condorcet's *Life of Turgot*. 'The heroic virtue of these glorious representatives of the opinions with which I sympathized, deeply affected me, and I perpetually recurred to them as others do to a favourite poet.' He similarly attributed his 'strong and permanent interest in Continental Liberalism' to a year's stay as a 14-year-old in France, and in particular to time spent in the house of his father's friend Jean Baptiste Say, 'a man of the later period of the French Revolution' and 'a fine specimen of the best kind of French republican … who had never bent the knee to Bonaparte … a truly upright, brave and enlightened man'.

As a result of the Reform Bill of 1832, several of the 'philosophical radicals' entered Parliament and seemed in 'a more advantageous position … for shewing what was in them'. But their achievements were disappointing. Not only did they do 'very little to promote any opinions', but they had to operate in 'ten years of inevitable reaction, when the Reform excitement being over and the few legislative improvements which the public really called for having been rapidly effected, power gravitated back in its natural direction, to those who were for keeping things as they were'.[53] Worse still, the predominant form of popular radicalism, what became known as Chartism and, as in France, now a movement of 'the working classes', moved decisively against them.

The relations between parliamentary radicals and the Chartist leader, Fergus O' Connor, denounced by them as 'a weak and cowardly demagogue', deteriorated to the point where in 1842 all effective collaboration ground to a halt. To denunciations of ancient radical enemies were added polemics against free trade and the middle classes; and in 1847 O'Connor actually stood for Parliament as a Tory. As the despairing leader of the Anti-Corn Law League, Richard Cobden, wrote to Joseph Sturge:

> The Chartists don't seem to understand their real position. They direct all their attacks against capital, machinery, manufactures and trade, which are the only materials of democracy, but they never assail the feudal aristocracy and the State Church which are the materials of the oligarchical despotism under which they are suffering. Fergus and his demoniacal followers seem bent on destroying manufacturers in order to restore the age of gothic feudalism.[54]

It was not entirely surprising that the ideas advanced by Mill and his allies commanded little popular support. Mill's radicalism was not simply aimed at aristocracy and church, it also linked the possibility of improvement with a change in the manners of the poor. Quite as important as anything put forward by Bentham was 'Malthus's population principle', 'a banner and point of union among us'. In Mill's view, 'this great doctrine', originally an argument against 'indefinite improveability of human affairs', was 'the sole means of realising that improveability by securing full employment at high wages to the whole labouring population through a voluntary restriction of the increase of their numbers'.[55]

It is true that, unlike Malthus, he was willing to advocate the use of contraception, which political debate had been inhibited from addressing by 'scrupulosity of speech'. But the moralism underpinning this preoccupation, which Mill retained throughout his life, was quite as intense as in the case of the 'industriousness' and 'frugality' enjoined by Say. 'Poverty,' Mill argued, 'like most social evils, exists because men follow their brute instincts without due consideration.' 'Civilisation' was a 'struggle against these animal instincts', though hampered yet again by the machinations of force and fraud. Mill thought that thoughtless parenthood should be treated like drunkenness. 'Little improvement can be expected in morality until the producing of large families is regarded with the same feelings as drunkenness or any other physical excess. But while the aristocracy and clergy are foremost to set the example of incontinence, what can be expected from the poor?'[56]

What was inadequate about the diagnoses of Mill, and before him Say, was the remoteness of their prescriptions from the specific, and to some extent novel, conditions of the nineteenth-century economy. Say's paen to industriousness went back to Father Abraham and mid-eighteenth century rural New England; Malthus's principle of population arguably explained the past better than the future and increasingly mistook symptom for cause (it is poverty that produces large families, rather than large families that produce poverty). In the 1790s, rising Poor Rates, rising grain prices, virtual famine conditions in 1795 and 1800 and the findings of the 1801 census all appeared to underline the urgency of Malthus's warnings. But thereafter, aside from an exceptional scarcity in western Europe in 1817, Malthus's doctrine appeared increasingly wide of the mark. The 1790s were the last years in which England (though not Ireland) was remotely threatened by famine conditions.

In this sense, the position which became identified with a liberal political economy, committed to the struggle of enlightenment against ignorance, aristocracy and church, appeared increasingly closed off from the newness and unfamiliarity of nineteenth-century economic crises. New perceptions and insights were more the province of mavericks, socialists or conservatives; and none more so than Thomas Carlyle, who, as Mill admitted, was 'a man of intuition' who 'saw many things long before me'. Like Owen and

Sismondi, and Charles Fourier in France, Carlyle discerned something new and strange in the nineteenth-century polarity between wealth and poverty, epitomised by the phenomenon of *over*production.

His most eloquent invocation of this phenomenon occurred at the beginning of *Past and Present*, in which he described the depression of 1842:

> The condition of England … is justly regarded as one of the most ominous, and withal one of the strangest, ever seen in this world. England is full of wealth, of multifarious produce, supply for human want in every kind; yet England is dying of inanition. With unabated bounty the land of England blooms and grows; waving with yellow harvests; thick-studded with workshops, industrial implements, with fifteen millions of workers, understood to be the strongest, the cunningest and the willingest our Earth ever had … This successful industry of England, with its plethoric wealth, has as yet made nobody rich; it is an enchanted wealth, and belongs yet to nobody … In the midst of plethoric plenty, the people perish; with gold walls and full barns, no man feels himself safe or satisfied … Midas longed for gold, and insulted the Olympians. He got gold, so that whatsoever he touched became gold – and he with his long ears, was little the better for it.[57]

But even apart from the newness of the poverty associated with machinery, cyclical depression, declining industries and the mass migration of laid-off agricultural workers or pauperised Irish peasants into the towns, the arguments of Say and Mill barely connected with the difficulties experienced daily by the new poor. The proposals of Condorcet and Paine had either been wholly forgotten or dismissed as wildly impractical. Blanqui consigned Condorcet namelessly to the wilder shores of the French Revolution:

> Did evil come from nature or society? Was it impossible to remedy or could it with the help of time be cured? Struck by what could be achieved by laws concerning the manners and conditions of peoples, eminent writers had thought that the miseries of man were of his own doing, and that it depended upon him to bring them to an end, much less by changing his passions than by changing political institutions. It was 1798. In France, a memorable experiment had been attempted, in just a few years, there had been witnessed the boldest reforms, applied in turn by reason or force, leave the human species at the mercy of the same uncertainties and the same inequalities as in the past. The division of properties had replaced the former system of concentration, power had been put into the hands of the poorest of the masses, who had denied themselves neither *the maximum*, nor the forced loans, nor bankruptcy, nor the suppression of indirect taxation; and yet the poor were still there, men dressed in rags, old people without bread, women without assistance, foundlings, malefactors and prostitutes. What remained to do after all that had been

done? What monarchy would attempt what could not be achieved by the audacities of 1793?[58]

As for Paine, his *Age of Reason* remained famous among freethinkers and his case against the exploitative role of taxation, put forward in *The Rights of Man*, remained part of the standard repertoire of popular radicalism. However, his social insurance proposals attracted little attention and no sustained commitment. A heroic biography published in 1821 by one of his most prominent freethinking admirers, Richard Carlile, was distinctly non-committal about his schemes for welfare. He did not mention the proposals in *The Rights of Man*, while on the plan for death duties in *Agrarian Justice*, he remarked, '[T]he idea was evidently the offspring of humanity and benevolence; of its practicability I cannot speak here, as nothing but experience could prove it.' Like Cobbett, he warmed far more to the more traditional attack on debt and paper money in *The Decline and Fall of the English System of Finance.*[59]

However impractical the social insurance proposals of Condorcet or Paine were sometimes claimed to be, in the face of the fluctuating and uncertain movements of the nineteenth-century economy it is difficult to argue that their expectations were less realistic than the contrasting hopes invested in 'industriousness', 'frugality' or reproductive foresight. These were qualities which presupposed regularity and predictability of earnings together with knowledge. Emphasis upon the manners of the people did not take sufficient account of the accompanying doctrine of 'the formation of all human character by circumstances'. In their reaction against the simple-minded and authoritarian legislative fantasies of the Jacobins, these radicals placed too little faith in the limited but real benefits attainable through institutional change.

Not enough attention was paid either not only to the obstacles created by lack of education, but also to the difficulties posed by the extent of underemployment and of seasonal and casual labour, both in the cities and in the countryside. This meant that savings banks were beyond the horizons of the poor, while birth control was shrouded in a fog of ignorance. Henry Mayhew estimated that 'in the generality of trades the calculation is that one third of the hands are fully employed, one third partially, and one third unemployed throughout the year'. 'All casual labour', he wrote, 'is necessarily uncertain labour; and wherever uncertainty exists, there can be no foresight or providence.' Or, as he observed in the course of his enquiry into London dock labourers: 'Where the means of subsistence occasionally rise to 15s. per week and occasionally sink to nothing, it's absurd to look for prudence, economy or moderation. Regularity of habits are incompatible with irregularity of income.'[60]

Membership of friendly societies was widespread and the growth of such societies in eighteenth- and nineteenth-century England was more pronounced than in France. Frederick Eden had estimated that membership of friendly societies already amounted to around 648,000 in 1801.

By 1872, the number had risen to around 4,000,000. J. M. Baernreither, an Austrian observer in the 1880s, praised the friendly societies for 'having propagated the conviction of the necessity of insurance among the working classes': 'Contributions to sick and burial societies form at the present day in England standing items even in the scanty budget of the working-men; the interest taken in Friendly Societies by working-men of all descriptions is universal ... The English workman regards with pride the Friendly Societies as his own work.'[61]

But it is important not to take too roseate a view of these institutions. For even where workers were in a position to save, the chances that their savings would remain safe were small. Before the 1870s, small local friendly societies were the only institutions available to most wage-earners, and the rate of failure of these societies was high. Until the mid-century expansion of nationwide affiliated orders, most societies were created in and often by public houses, contained less than 200 members, and met in pub rooms, for which members paid rent in the form of the purchase of a prearranged quantity of 'lodge liquor'. Members held office in rotation, irrespective of talent, and so, not surprisingly, there was little or no knowledge of the actuarial basis of premiums. The fixing of benefits and contributions was largely established by local custom, but was also affected by the competition between rival pub-promoted local schemes. New societies offered extra inducements: larger contributions in drink on club nights or indefinite sick pay at full benefit instead of graduated reductions. The most frequently cited reason for failure was simply the offering of too much benefit in return for too little contribution. In addition, little account was taken of the age structure of the membership, which often meant that men who had joined in clusters in their twenties found themselves cast adrift from a failing club after twenty years as demands for sickness benefit began to increase. Henceforward, however, they would be unprotected against sickness and old age, since forty was generally taken as the upper age limit for new members.

In 1819, the government attempted to make these societies more secure by requiring Justices of the Peace to refuse to register a society unless it had submitted tables and rules approved by 'two persons at the least known to be professional actuaries or persons skilled in calculation'. But, as a select committee of the Commons of 1825 discovered, local expertise of this kind was not widespread. Approval was, therefore, entrusted to 'petty schoolmasters and accountants whose opinion about the probability of sickness, and the duration of life is not to be depended upon'.[62]

Yet even if the most diligent enquiries had been made, no reliable estimates of rates of sickness were available until after the middle of the century. Furthermore, given the small numbers in such societies, actuarial knowledge would not have been especially valuable. Average rates of sickness varied widely from trade to trade and from region to region, and an epidemic could wipe out or disable a large proportion of the local membership. By the 1870s, the situation had significantly improved. The majority of local societies had been incorporated into the large and stable affiliated orders which by then were in possession of considerable financial and actuarial expertise. But this process had been very slow. Even in 1872, not much more than half the registered societies provided details of their membership. One of the assistant commissioners to the Royal Commission on Friendly Societies, reporting on Oldham, found 230 societies, nearly all of whom had spent funds on convivial purposes, lacked sound management and were now nearly all 'insolvent in the more obvious and painful sense … of now failing to pay the benefits they have promised'.[63] There could scarcely be a better advertisement for 'the law of large numbers' or for Condorcet's 'calculus of probabilities'.

VI

RESOLVING
'THE SOCIAL PROBLEM'

For Paine and Condorcet in the 1790s, the elimination of
poverty had been part of a pitched battle between advancing enlightenment and the receding defences of 'force
and fraud'. These powers were personified by the aristocracy and the established church. In this battle, the works
of Adam Smith had been a crucial asset. In the eyes of his
progressive followers of the 1780s and 1790s, Smith's great
achievement had not only been to spell out the historical
and political importance of the progress of exchange, but
also to distinguish the peaceful and reciprocally beneficial
facets of exchange from the self-interested pleading of merchants, feudal magnates, closed corporations, mercantilist
politicians and religious establishments. Commerce – the
unhampered transactions between individuals desirous of
bettering their condition – would no longer be weighed
down and misshapen by the burdens imposed upon it by
vested interests and the residues of a feudal past. Having
been made accountable to the deliberations of representative and democratic bodies, assisted by the free circulation

of knowledge, and nurtured by peaceful and non-predatory government, its benign potential would freely unfold.

Commerce, in its eighteenth-century sense, also conveyed a certain mode of sociability. In the usage of Hume and Montesquieu, commerce implied peaceableness and the 'polishing' of manners. The French and American Revolutions added a further dimension. This sociability would now be practised by citizens sufficiently equal in legal and material status to possess moral and intellectual independence in their transactions with each other. In other words, viewed by Condorcet and Paine, the commerce of the future assumed dimensions which were at the same time both liberal and republican.

In the long nineteenth century which followed the Revolution of 1789, it was to be expected that such an approach would be more likely to find a home in a republic, such as that established and consolidated in France in the decades after 1870. In Britain, not only was the power of the crown, in a symbolic if not a constitutional sense, enormously boosted by the upsurge of loyalism after 1789, but the political privileges and wealth of the aristocracy remained undiminished until the end of the 1870s.

The intermittently stormy post-revolutionary history of France in the decades between the 1830s and the 1880s – and beyond – meant that, even in the Third Republic, ideas about the social underpinnings of a republic rarely had the chance to become established. Either they were overshadowed by more pressing political concerns or they were surrounded by a legacy of fear and suspicion which the revolutions and uprisings of 1830, 1848 and 1871 could only reinforce. For this reason, legislative enactments to give reality to a social republican vision came only several decades into the history of the Third Republic and were relatively limited in their practical effects.

In the first months of the 1848 revolution, for instance, the dreams of 'association' emanating from 'the parliament of labour' at the Luxembourg Palace in Paris were lumped together by legitimists, conservatives and liberals alike as symptoms of anarchy and disorder. The bad reputation of the national workshops for the unemployed of Paris in bourgeois and provincial France and its culmination in the June uprising of 1848 quickly killed off any temptation to further social experiment. Thiers expressed the sentiments of the majority of the National Assembly when he stated on 13 September 1848:

> All that has been found to replace the old principles of the former society, of society in every age, in every country – property, liberty (of labour), emulation or competition, all that has been found, is communism, that is to say the lazy and slavish society; association, that is to say, anarchy in industry, and monopoly, the suppression of the currency and the right to work. [1]

The anti-interventionist individualism of Orleanist liberals like Thiers expressed the viewpoint of the propertied classes across France. Or, as Frederick Bastiat put it, 'What political economy asks of governments is as simple as the retort of Diogenes to Alexander: get out of my sunlight'.

Liberal notables were scarcely less hostile to Bonaparte's promises of a social progamme. In 1844, the future Napoleon III had written a pamphlet on *The Extinction of Pauperism*. Its argument was that it was necessary to turn the property-less working class into proprietors and that through 'association' in the form of 'agricultural colonies', 'poverty will no longer be seditious'. Tocqueville characterised his approach as 'a sort of abstract adoration of the people' unaccompanied by 'any taste for liberty'. During the Second Empire, Napoleon took a spasmodic interest in the mobilisation and support of mutual benefit societies, but never without the heavy hand of administrative and political surveillance. Not surprisingly, these plans got nowhere in practice.

In effect, whatever the nature of the political regime at the centre, social services remained almost entirely a local responsibility. The day-to-day functioning of offices of public assistance, hospitals, *dépôts de mendicité*, orphanages, mental asylums, the regulation of apprenticeship and child labour, the monitoring of benefit societies and sanitary regulation were divided between communes and *départements*. The Ministry of the Interior, the Ministry of Commerce and various specialised governmental agencies, oversaw developments in these areas, but at least until the 1890s did not directly intervene or offer material support. There was nothing comparable to the proactive ambitions of direction and control by central government such as those pursued by the Poor Law Commissioners and Local Government Board in Victorian England.[2]

In the first two decades of the Third Republic there was little discernible change in these arrangements. On social and economic questions, the so-called 'Opportunists' who governed the Republic from the end of the 1870s differed little from their Orleanist predecessors. Unlike the religious and the legitimists, they were not shaken by the Commune, which they regarded as an aberration. Like their moderate republican predecessors from Thermidor onwards, they preached a somewhat short-winded moralism, stressing hygiene, sobriety, saving and economy; and still followed the precepts of Benjamin Franklin's *Le Bonhomme Richard* (*Poor Richard's Almanack*), which Jean-Baptiste Say had recommended in *Olbie*.

There was, however, one major area in which the approach of even the most moderate republicans differed from that of the monarchists and the Catholics, and in which the legacy of Condorcet remained very much alive. Almost all republicans were agreed about the central role to be played by education in the new republic. Education was important because, as Ferdinand Buisson wrote of Ferry's educational reforms in 1882: 'When the whole of French youth has developed, grown up under this triple aegis of free, compulsory, secular education we shall have nothing more to fear from returns to the past, for we shall have the means of defending ourselves.' Education was central not simply because it would mould the people into the ethos of the Republic, but also because all except a small minority of republicans believed that it would be the means of creating equality and bringing to an end the social hierarchies of the past.

A more decisive shift in attitudes, at least among radical republicans, occurred in the 1890s with the emergence in the political arena of the doctrine of 'solidarism'. This concept was put forward by Leon Bourgeois, briefly prime minister in 1895–6, in his book *La Solidarité*, which appeared in 1896 and was adopted by the Radical Party as the basis of its party programme in 1908.

Solidarism owed something to the socialist thought of the 1830s but much more to a positivist optimism about the role of scientific progress, in particular the hopes invested in a science of society. Most immediately, Bourgeois built upon the theories of Émile Durkheim, especially the arguments put forward in his book *The Division of Labour* (1893) and developed in *Suicide* (1897). Durkheim believed it possible to build a science of morality and, in *The Division of Labour* he laid out some of its foundations. He distinguished between the 'mechanical' solidarity characteristic of primitive societies and the 'organic' solidarity characteristic of an evolved society based upon the division of labour.

The apparent paradox of the division of labour, in Durkheim's view, was that while the individual became more autonomous in an evolved society, at the same time s\he also became more narrowly dependent upon that society. Unlike the automatic 'mechanical' solidarity of primitive society, in which the idea of the autonomous individual did not exist, there was nothing automatic about the 'organic' solidarity needed in societies based upon the division of labour. In evolved societies, such 'solidarity' had to be constructed through the elaboration of a body of rules which bound the component parts of such societies together. Like Condorcet, Durkheim built upon an anti-Rousseauean position, emphasising that modern society could not maintain itself without a series of intermediate bodies, especially professional associations capable of integrating individuals. Such a society would nurture the idea that social existence was a moral whole and that it depended for its development upon mutual sacrifice.[3]

Bourgeois's aim was to turn Durkheim's arguments to practical political use. Opposing the idea of a state of nature, Bourgeois argued that man was born 'in debt' to human association. From birth, he benefited from the past inheritance of a society and was in turn a link in the chain of solidarity which bound society together. Just as society created ties of dependence, this social debt created a moral obligation. He conceived of this unspoken obligation as a quasi-contract. Had the individual been consulted at the moment of entry into the world, he or she would surely have recognised that debt. The state as the guardian of law should encourage, or even, by means of taxation, constrain individuals to recognise these social obligations towards the collectivity. Practically, the state should discharge the debt owed to society by taking care of children, the sick and the old and pay for this care by means of a progressive income tax. Both Durkheim and Bourgeois were careful, however, to argue that solidarism did not entail the activity of an overbearing interventionist state. The ties of obligation were generated by free associations acting within civil society. The role of the state was to protect them and support them by means of material assistance.

In his brief term as prime minister in 1895, Bourgeois tried, unsuccessfully, to introduce income tax to support what he called 'sensible practical socialism', and in the following decade a series of social measures were enacted. These included industrial accident insurance in 1898, the regulation of working hours in 1900, death duties in 1901, a weekly rest day in 1906 and old age pensions in 1910. But, as Madeleine Rebérioux and J. M. Mayeur have argued, 'the system was extremely sluggish; it had taken twenty years to pass the law on pensions, and twenty years, too, for the tax on income, "the Sleeping Beauty tax"'.[4]

Support for these measures by their intended beneficiaries was tepid. Organised labour led by the Confédération Générale des Travailleurs (General Confederation of Workers) campaigned against the law on pensions, not only because of its derisory character, but also because the workers did not trust 'the robber state'. Both pensions and income tax were blocked for a considerable time by the Senate. The Contributory Pensions Act, which was supposed to apply to workers and peasants, was considered a 'fiasco'. Traditional republicans had great misgivings about the introduction of compulsion, since it implied the acceptance of a society permanently divided into classes and the abandonment of the idea that the worker could aspire to independence. Even among the radicals at their Nancy Conference of 1907, the social programme designed to attract the support of workers was coupled to a vision of 'the end of the wage system' and the ability to 'obtain access to individual property, which is the true condition of its [the proletariat's] liberty and dignity'.[5]

~

In Britain, as well, there was a shift in attitudes towards poverty during the last twenty years of the nineteenth century. But the positions adopted in the resultant political debate could not have been predicted from the struggles of the 1790s. For the heirs to Painite republicanism and secularism combined these positions with an intransigent defence of Malthus and individualism. By contrast, the Church of England, or at least the leading reforming current within it, attacked political economy for its individualism and hostility to trade unions.

Some developments, however, might have been foreseen. By the 1870s, steamships and the telegraph had transformed the pace of commercial transactions, while railways had opened up the interiors of vast and hitherto inaccessible continents. The pessimistic prophecies of protectionists at the time of the repeal of the Corn Laws in 1846 were finally

beginning to come true, as the fall in world prices hit agriculture and began to undermine the wealth and power of
the aristocracy. Cobden and the Anti-Corn Law League had
won a belated victory, since the strength of Free Trade sentiment meant that, in Britain at least, the dramatic decline of
cereal prices after 1870 was not accompanied by the return
of protection.

At the beginning of the 1880s, great landowners, particularly those with urban property, also found their wealth and
power under attack from a new form of popular radicalism. Once more, as in the case of Paine nearly a century
before, it was a radical inspired by a vision of America who
had transformed the terms of political debate: 'If we had to
assign to any one event the starting of the new current of
thought', wrote Sidney Webb in 1890, 'we should name the
wide circulation in Great Britain of Henry George's *Progress
and Poverty* during the years 1880–1882.'[6] On the basis of his
experiences in California, Henry George attacked Malthus,
holding that the unearned increment of the landlord was
responsible for the poverty of the masses. As soon as practicable, he argued, the land must be made common property,
while in the interim a single tax should be imposed upon
land values. Not only did his book sell over 100,000 copies
but, in several tours of Britain in the early 1880s, his powerful
oratory left a lasting impact.

In some important ways, Henry George's arguments
appeared like a return to the pre-Malthusian perspectives
of the late Enlightenment reformers. 'Social development,'

he argued in *Progress and Poverty*, 'is governed neither by a Special Providence nor by a merciless fate, but by a law at once unchangeable and beneficent; when we see that human will is the great factor, and that taking men in the aggregate, their condition is as they make it; when we see that economic and moral law are essentially one, and that the truth which the intellect grasps after toilsome effort is but that which the moral sense reaches by a quick intuition, a flood of life breaks in upon the problem of individual life.'[7] George's assault upon 'the unearned increment' and his proposal of a single tax on land helped to make possible Sir William Harcourt's 1894 budget, which introduced death duties. This measure, as Moncure Conway remarked in his pioneer biography of Paine, had been anticipated by the proposals in *Agrarian Justice* a hundred years earlier.

But such continuities are also deceptive. Although Henry George defined 'the law of progress' as 'association in equality', his starting point was closer to Ricardo and the early works of Herbert Spencer than to the arguments of the 1790s. *Progress and Poverty* made no mention of Paine or Condorcet and showed no interest in 'the calculus of probabilities'. Its radicalism was based upon a simple reading of Ricardo's theory of rent, in which the gains from the progress of society went exclusively to the rentier at the expense of both worker and employer. George's starting point was 'the squalid misery of a great city', which he and his followers linked to the undiminished power and wealth of the aristocracy as ground landlords in the towns.[8]

The best-known guardians of the tradition of Painite radicalism in British politics in the 1870s and 1880s were the activists of the Secularist movement, in particular, their leader, the editor of the *National Reformer*, Charles Bradlaugh. For Secularists, Paine's most revered text was *The Age of Reason*, a deist attack on Christianity. But Bradlaugh, like Paine and Richard Carlile, combined the campaign for Free Thought with that of republican radicalism. He believed, like Paine, that 'for free and rational men the only right form of Government is a Republic' and his aim, like that of his predecessors, according to his daughter, Hypatia Bonner, was 'the bringing of reason to bear at once on the things of Church and of State'.

But on questions of social welfare, Bradlaugh was a dedicated follower of Malthus; so much so that in 1861 he had become secretary of the Malthusian League. For Bradlaugh, Malthus had correctly identified the fundamental cause of poverty. His only defect was his adherence to a Christian ethic. 'Neo-Malthusianism', as it was called, meant combining Malthus's 'principle of population' with the 'rationalist' conviction that 'the prudential check need not mean prolonged celibacy'. In other words, Bradlaugh advocated birth control. After challenging the law by republishing a 40-year-old birth control pamphlet entitled *Fruits of Philosophy: An Essay on the Population Question*, Bradlaugh and Annie Besant were arrested and prosecuted in a celebrated trial in 1877–8.

Bradlaugh had first laid out his position in 1861 in a

pamphlet entitled *Jesus, Shelley and Malthus*, in which he had sketched out three successive attitudes towards poverty: the spirit of religious submission; the spirit of humanitarian revolt; and the spirit of science. Like Mill, Bradlaugh considered that there could be no escape from poverty until the poor had been educated on the necessity of family limitation. He accordingly condemned Paine's social proposals. 'The plan of allowancing poor families at so much per head would have quickened immensely the progress towards national bankruptcy which was carried so far under the old Poor Law. It would have bred paupers by the thousand.' Nor was it surprising that in the 1880s he should have stepped forward as the chief oratorical opponent of socialism and of Henry George. 'In a Socialistic State,' Bradlaugh argued in 1884, 'there would be no inducement to thrift, no individual savings, no accumulation, no check upon waste.'[9]

The welfare legislation of the Liberal governments of 1906–14 owed nothing to the ideas of Paine or Condorcet. The informing vision was no longer cosmopolitan, but national and imperial. The primary concern within government appears to have been the military and industrial efficiency of a working population now threatened by the competition of foreign powers.[10] Not surprisingly, at a time when Queen Victoria had become Empress of India and the scramble for Africa had reached its height, there was little place for a discussion whose prime aim in the ending of poverty was to create a republic of educated and independent citizens.

The case for 'national insurance' had first been proposed by the Reverend W. E. Blackley in 1878. He made no reference to the 1790s or the French Revolution. His aim was not to further equality, but to improve upon the New Poor Law of 1834 which, despite the improvements of the 1860s, had failed to reduce pauperism beyond a certain point. Blackley's proposal involved a scheme to 'abolish the improvidence, which is the curse, and, unchecked, must become the ruin, of our nation'. He argued that 'to make a reasonable provision against occasional sickness and the inevitable feebleness and infirmity of old age' was 'the duty of every man gifted with health and strength, and in a position to earn, by his daily labour, a wage from which such provision' could 'be made'. But this 'universally admitted duty' remained 'grossly neglected by our working classes'.

Blackley claimed that many friendly societies were insolvent, that withdrawals from benefit societies amounted to at least half the number of entries made in any particular year, and that a substantial proportion of these withdrawals – particularly those from people in middle life – were permanent. The final and most telling point was that 'the rates of payment which can really assure the benefits generally offered by friendly societies are far higher than any ordinary labourer in middle life can find it possible to pay'. The net result was that, 'if every friendly society in England were perfectly solvent, and if all that the law contemplated and all that philanthropy suggested had been completely realised there would still remain 75% of the labouring classes entirely dependent, in emergencies upon the poor rate, and therefore to be classed as improvident paupers'.

His solution was to make thrift compulsory. Every working man between the ages of eighteen and twenty-one should contribute £10 to an annuity fund, a 'national club', and payments should be made through employers or through the Post Office. The labouring classes should be shown how to contribute, and if they would not, they should be 'compelled' to do so. His response to those who objected to a compulsory state scheme was to point out how extensive state intervention in everyday life already was: 'A man who trembles so at the thought of any interference with his liberty, knows, if he will reflect a moment, that it is interfered with terribly when he is compelled to make his cottages fit for habitation; is compelled to disinfect his clothes if he has had the small-pox; is compelled to have his baby vaccinated; is compelled to keep it off the streets; is compelled, mayhap, to send it to a board school, and is even compelled, if need unhappily be, to pay for its support in a reformatory.'[11]

Blackley's argument was exaggerated. He made no attempt to understand the position of the friendly societies, and his estimate of £10 seriously underestimated the sum needed to yield an old age pension. Nevertheless, in the mid-twentieth century, the sequence of events which ran from Blackley's proposal to the 1908 Old Age Pensions Act and the National Insurance Act of 1911 was depicted as a progression from a coercive, moralistic and discretionary

Poor Law relief system towards a liberal welfare state, universal in coverage, morally neutral in application, democratic in administration and based on legally enforceable social rights.[12]

It is true that pressure for state-supported *non*-contributory pension schemes did build up among the trade unions and the Lib–Lab MPs elected in 1906. Their arguments were also reinforced by the influential advocacy of Charles Booth, who had argued for a non-contributory scheme at the beginning of the 1890s. But the legislation of the Liberal governments between 1908 and 1911 was far less of a break with Poor Law tradition than the mid-twentieth century historians implied. Except in the case of old age pensions, the spirit of this legislation was anything but universalistic. Women, except in a few designated employments, were excluded from health and unemployment insurance, and so were the bulk of male wage-earners in casual employment. Nor did the legislation make any pretence of aspiring to moral neutrality or a democratic inclusiveness. Pressure in shaping the legislation came primarily from the friendly societies, the Charity Organisation Society and the commercial insurance companies.

The whole principle of social insurance was regarded with great suspicion by the Charity Organisation Society and its sympathisers in the ministry responsible for the Poor Law, the Local Government Board. Their view was that it was impossible to 'legislate thrift' and that there should be no retreat from the strict deterrent principles of the 1834 Poor Law. As a result, except in the case of old age pensions, the Liberal welfare reforms brought into being a set of institutions which did not replace the Poor Law, but ran alongside it. The unexpectedly non-contributory form of the 1908 Old Age Pensions Act was the result not so much of parliamentary or trade union pressure, but of the opposition of the friendly societies to any state-enforced contributory proposal.

The power of the friendly societies was greater than that of either the Charity Organisation Society or the Local Government Board. Their membership was twice as large as that of the trade unions and their political influence was such that no politician, either in Westminster or in the country, dared to oppose them. Their objection to both Blackley's contributory scheme and a similar proposal put forward by Joseph Chamberlain in 1891, was that they would be competing in the same limited market for working-class savings as the friendly societies themselves. With ageing memberships living longer, but drawing ever more heavily upon society sickness benefits as surrogate pensions, many of these societies, especially the smaller ones, appeared to be headed for insolvency. By contrast, the 1908 Act, which paid old age pensions out of general taxation, helped the societies by removing some of the pressure on their sickness benefits and muted their anxieties about the involvement of the state.

While the Liberal government overcame its misgivings about financing an old age pensions scheme of unknown cost, it was not prepared to extend such a non-contributory approach to sickness or unemployment. Once again, it seems that the thinking behind the National Insurance Act of 1911 did not draw in any way upon the forgotten social insurance proposals of the French Revolutionary era. The chief influence upon Lloyd George, the minister responsible for the scheme, appears to have been the social legislation of Bismarckian Germany between 1883 and 1889. These measures included accident insurance, sickness benefit and old age pensions, each to be financed in different proportions by contributions from employees, employers and government.

In Germany itself, the legislation had largely been a development of the practice of employer welfare schemes in big industrial enterprises such as the Krupp works in Essen and the Stumm-Halberg works in the Saar. In Britain, however, the emphasis was rather different. Domestically, the main aim was to ensure that workers should not fall involuntarily into a pauper non-citizen category for reasons over which they had no personal control. For this reason, unlike in Germany, benefits were not graduated, but set at a flat rate high enough to make it unnecessary for workers to resort to the Poor Law.[13]

Great care was also taken to incorporate friendly societies within the scheme, an approach which produced many kinds of anomalies and a form of coverage which was neither universal nor free from moralism. Friendly societies retained their rules, which generally included a range of highly censorious provisions against malingerers. They were also able to refuse applicants, potentially perpetuating the same kind of problems which had left the bottom third of the working classes outside the insured population during the Victorian period. The problem was partly solved by the entry of industrial and life insurance companies into the sickness insurance business, but their inclusion was at the cost of the tradition of local and democratic self-government originally intended to be the hallmark of the 1911 Act.

The most coherent and historically informed of the new conceptions of social security which emerged in the late nineteenth century was that adopted by liberal reformers within the Church of England. It both helped to inspire the late Victorian settlement movement and made a major contribution to the new liberalism of the turn of the century. One of its most important activists was Samuel Barnett, the vicar of St Jude's, Whitechapel, and first warden of Toynbee Hall. He recalled that he had arrived in his parish in 1873, convinced by the arguments of the newly founded Charity Organisation Society that 'doles' given in the shape either of charity or outrelief 'did not make the poor any richer, but served rather to perpetuate poverty'. This victory was won, outrelief to the able-bodied in Whitechapel was abolished and charity only given in conjunction with the careful investigation of individual circumstances.[14] But by 1883 he declared himself not happy with the results. The labourer in middle life on 20s. per week, he wrote, 'hardly dares to think', for, given the insecurity of employment in east London, 'in the labourer's future there are only the workhouse and the grave'. But even with a skill and 40s. per week, there was no margin 'out of which to provide for pleasure, for old age or even for the best medical skill'. England, he went on, 'is the land of sad monuments. The saddest monument is, perhaps, "the respectable working man", who has been erected in honour of Thrift. His brains, which might have shown the world how to save men, have been spent in saving pennies.'

Because of their lack of an adequate standard of living, the lives of the majority of the English population were poor, materially, and even more important, spiritually. They were excluded from the world of culture and beauty:

> To live the life of Christ is to make manifest the truth and to enjoy the beauty of God. The labourer who knows nothing of the law of life which has been revealed by the discoveries of science, who knows nothing which by admiration can lift him out of himself, cannot live the highest life of his day, as Christ lived the highest life of his day. The social reformer must go alongside the Christian missionary.

He, therefore, proposed a programme of social reform which included old age pensions, schools of industry, medical relief, adult education, libraries, gardens and a more sensitive approach to the problem of slum clearance.[15]

Such an approach had already been pioneered by the young Balliol tutor and Christian activist Arnold Toynbee.

Toynbee remains famous not only for the new charitable settlement which bears his name but also as the historian who first introduced the idea of 'the industrial revolution' into English discussion. His *Lectures on the Industrial Revolution in England*, together with some addresses on political economy and contemporary politics, were edited by his friend, the future South African pro-consul Alfred Milner, and introduced by the Master of Balliol, Benjamin Jowett. In the *Lectures*, Toynbee refers to Marx's *Capital* (which he probably read in French translation), Henry George, Sismondi and Lassalle, as well as more familiar British sources, especially Thomas Carlyle. 'The essence of the Industrial Revolution,' according to Toynbee, who dated its beginnings to the 1760s, 'was the substitution of competition for medieval regulations, which had previously controlled the production and distribution of wealth.' Its ethos, 'freedom' as 'the first and last word of the political and industrial philosophy of the age', had been proclaimed on the 'eve of the Industrial Revolution' by Adam Smith. 'When Adam Smith talked with James Watt in his workshop at Glasgow, he little thought that by the steam engine Watt would make possible the realisation of that freedom which Adam Smith looked upon as a dream, a utopia.'

Toynbee was struck by Smith's 'cosmopolitanism', which had provoked his attack on the mercantile system, but especially by Smith's 'primary axiom' that 'men follow their pecuniary interest'. 'Equally prominent', however, was Smith's 'individualism', 'his complete and unhesitating trust in individual self-interest'. This axiom had been developed to its furthest extent in the political economy of Ricardo:

> That world of gold-seeking animals, stripped of every human affection, for ever digging, weaving, spinning, watching with keen undeceived eyes each other's movements, passing incessantly and easily from place to place in search of gain, all alert, crafty, mobile – that world less real than the island of Lilliput which has never had and never can have any existence.

It had been Smith's conviction that 'the individual in pursuing his own interest is promoting the welfare of all'. Smith was 'interested in the production of wealth, not the welfare of man'. He did not recognise that the principle of *laisser faire* 'breaks down in certain points'. Not only could there be conflicts of interest between consumers and producers, but also 'a permanent antagonism of interests in the distribution of wealth … where the harmony of the individual and the public interest is a figment'. These antagonisms emerged more strongly after Smith's time in 'a darker period … as disastrous and terrible as any through which a nation ever passed … because side by side with a great increase of wealth was seen an enormous increase of pauperism'. Furthermore, 'production on a vast scale, the result of free competition, led to a rapid alienation of classes and to the degradation of a large body of producers'. Toynbee went on to support this claim with an account of the decline of the yeoman, the factory system in conjunction with 'the all-corroding force of foreign trade, the growth of the farmers as a class distinct from their labourers who were henceforth "expelled and degraded", and in the manufacturing world, the separation of masters and men in which a "cash nexus" was substituted for the human tie'.[16]

In politics, according to Jowett, Toynbee was 'not a party politician at all'. 'He was not a socialist or a democrat, though he had some tendencies in both directions.' He followed Marx's *Capital* in thinking of the 'free exchange of labour' as the crucial component in the emergence of modern industry, but described Adam Smith's enunciation of this doctrine in the language of Carlyle's denunciation of 'the cash nexus'. He also followed Coleridge in arguing that the tendency of political economy was to 'denationalise'. Mill's distinction between production and distribution and his late abandonment of the wage–fund theory enabled him to express 'his strong natural sympathy with the life of the labouring classes' and argue for the virtues and necessity of trade unions.

Yet in other respects, like Barnett, Toynbee remained true to his Charity Organisation Society formation, especially in his treatment of pauperism. The New Poor Law of 1834 was 'perhaps the most beneficial Act of Parliament which has been passed since the Reform Bill'. He blamed the landowners for an 'unthinking and ignorant benevolence' and, like Malthus, considered that there had been 'the growth of a sentiment which admitted an unconditional right on the part of the poor to an indefinite share in the national wealth'. This 'right' was granted in such a way as to 'keep them in dependence and diminish their self-respect'. He rejected this 'Tory socialism' and agreed with Burke's denunciation of the term 'labouring poor'. The Speenhamland system was an intimidatory use of its supposed 'rights' by the poor. 'The whole character of the people was lowered by the admission that they had a right to relief independent of work.'

Toynbee agreed with the socialists about the need for a more equitable distribution of wealth. 'Competition, heralded by Adam Smith, and taken for granted by Ricardo and Mill,' Toynbee wrote, 'is still the dominant idea of our time; though since the publication of the *Origin of Species*, we hear more of it under the name of "struggle for existence".' Henry George, he continued, was right to object to this analogy between men and animals and plants. To the idea that 'this struggle for existence' is a law of nature, and that therefore 'all human interference with it is wrong', Toynbee objected that 'the whole meaning of civilisation' was 'interference with this brute struggle'. Competition in production needed to be distinguished from competition in distribution which could be improved by political intervention.

Most noticeable in the writings of Toynbee and Barnett about poverty and the working classes was the disappearance of the Malthusian threat. Its dangers were diminished by a combination of free trade, informal empire and social reform. Toynbee noted that, despite Mill's insistence upon restriction of population as a precondition of improvement, the rate of increase had not slackened. But the burden this placed upon the supply of labour had been lightened by 'the enormous emigration' of three and a half million people since 1846. The outlook for the labourer was hopeful because 'there is no reason to suppose that there will be any check on this relief of the labourer for the next fifty years at least'.

At home, on the other hand, a programme of social reform was required. 'For the labouring masses, with whom prudential motives have no weight, the only true remedy is to carry out such great measures of social reform as the improvement of their dwellings, better education and better amusements, and thus lift them into the position now held by the artisan, where moral restraints are operative.' But a 'more equitable distribution of wealth' could only be attained coincidentally with moral progress. 'The old economists thought competition good in itself. The socialist thinks it an evil in itself ... we accept competition as one means, a force to be used, not to be blindly worshipped; but assert religion and morality to be the necessary condition of attaining human welfare.' As Jowett wrote, 'The Church of the future which Toynbee had before his mind was the union of the whole nation, or at least of the intelligent classes, in one body for a common purpose; mastering their own circumstances, and fellow workers towards a common end.'[17]

CONCLUSION

The argument put forward in *An End to Poverty?* is that the
first practicable proposals to eliminate poverty through the
creation of a universal framework for social security date
back to the 1790s, and were a direct product of the American
and French Revolutions. These were not proposals to resolve
the 'social problem', as that problem came to be understood
in the nineteenth and twentieth centuries. The purpose of
the schemes discussed by Condorcet and Paine was not to
remove the hostility of the working classes towards private
property or to overcome the antagonism between labour
and capital, since these were not yet perceived as intractable
problems. Social and political proposals went together, since
the aim was not solely to alleviate the lot of the poor but
to reproduce on European soil the conditions of existence
of a viable commercial republic akin to United States. All
would be citizens since an ignorant and dependent poor left
outside the political system would be vulnerable to faction
or demagogy, and a danger to the republic.

These proposals were products of a revolution which not

only overthrew the monarchy in France but toppled its aristocracy and unsettled their peers across Europe. Similarly, the new social programmes associated with the Revolution not only posed a direct challenge to the institutional role of the Catholic church in the provision of poor relief in France, but also directly threatened traditional Christian assumptions about poverty and charity in Britain as well. As the Revolution developed, it also became clear that the threat of the Revolution was not simply to the power, privileges and abuses of the Catholic church, but to the whole Christian cosmology throughout Europe and the wider world.

The fall of Robespierre, the famine of 1795 and the practical bankruptcy of the Jacobin state led to the wholesale abandonment of schemes to abolish mendicity. The administrative practices of Thermidor fell back once more upon pre-revolutionary forms of relief. After Napoleon's Concordat, the church also hastened to retrieve as much as it could of the charitable and educational sphere, which had traditionally belonged to it. Even among republicans, large-scale experiments in the abolition of mendicity were hastily forgotten. In their place there was once again a recycling of the homilies of Benjamin Franklin on questions of industry and thrift. This approach persisted among moderate republican leaders and their rural and small town supporters well into the twentieth century. Towards the end of the nineteenth century there were impressive attempts to rethink a republican notion of interdependence and social obligation, most notably in the work of Durkheim. But the practical results of the attempts by Leon Bourgeois and the Radical party to develop from this work a 'solidarist' political philosophy and legislative programme were relatively feeble.

In Britain, Paine's proposals reached and fired the enthusiasm of unparalleled numbers of people in a country still recovering from its American defeat, already in the middle of a religious revival and about to enter a counter-revolutionary war. Paine's mockery of his country's political institutions from the monarchy downwards was regarded with horror by the increasingly fearful and incensed loyalists and defenders of the existing state. But it was his undeniable popularity which caused most alarm. This was why the reaction was so intense.

The effort to thwart this revolutionary subversion of beliefs demanded the mobilisation of unprecedented numbers of the population and engaged the energies of every organ of church and state in every locality. More lastingly, this period of fear and uncertainty stamped upon the still protean features of political economy or Smith's 'science of the legislator' a deeply anti-utopian cast of mind, transforming future enquiry in the area into a gloomy and tirelessly repeated catechism, all too appropriate to what was becoming known as 'the dismal science'. The frisson of Smith's mild mockery of the manners of the great was gone. Instead, the ambition to combat poverty was henceforward conceived as a bleakly individual battle against the temptations of the flesh. Among the poor, even the procreation of children *within* marriage – though it could hardly be made punishable by eternal damnation – became the occasion of official and ecclesiastical eyebrow-raising when such activity was not attended by the due amount of prudence and foresight. This combination of evangelical prurience and Malthusian alarm provided much of the underpinnings of the Victorian attitude to sex.

So deep was the repression of this brief republican moment in modern British history that memory of it – or at least discussion of it among the governing classes – all but disappeared. By the Victorian era and certainly from the withering away of Chartism after 1848, it appeared as if there never had been a time – at least, not since Cromwell – when Britain's monarchy and its mixed constitution had come under serious threat. Paine was remembered for his attack on taxation and paper money, not for his republican social proposals. Republicanism in Victorian and Edwardian Britain was the concern of a shrill sect led by men like Bradlaugh, preaching atheism and sexual profligacy on the streets of London and Northampton, but also less open to Paine's social proposals than their Anglican counterparts. The dark period in British history around the years of Trafalgar and Waterloo was never entirely forgotten. But ultimately, an alternative story of Britain's ordeal was devised. It was a story powerful enough to provide the starting point of the social history of modern Britain, imparting to national, religious and economic concerns a historical form which was to endure through most of the twentieth century.

This was the significance of Arnold Toynbee's *Industrial*

Revolution, an eclectic masterpiece drawing its inspiration in equal measure from Thomas Carlyle, Karl Marx and the Charity Organisation Society, yet at the same time truly a prototype of G. M. Trevelyan's later definition of social history as 'history with the politics left out'. It is striking that in *The Industrial Revolution* the French Revolution is barely mentioned. Toynbee is too honest a historian to suppress historical material altogether. He cites the Marquis of Lansdowne's statement on 1 February 1793 in which Adam Smith was accused of being 'the real originator' of 'the French principles' against which a crusade was contemplated. He calls it 'a curious statement'. He makes no mention of Paine and maintains that it was not Godwin but the growth of pauperism which was 'the real cause' of Malthus's *Essay on Population*.

The republican challenge to the English constitution and the church was ignored. Instead, there was the 'industrial revolution', not only 'one of the most important facts of English history', but Europe owed to it 'the growth of two great systems of thought, economic science and its antithesis, socialism'. 'Economic science' meant Smith's 'gospel of industrial freedom' supplemented by Malthus on pauperism, Ricardo on rent and John Stuart Mill on distribution. If the radicalisation of British politics in the 1790s and the intensity of the conservative reaction did not concern Toynbee, it was because the die had already been cast. The sequence which led to the substitution of the 'cash nexus' for 'the human tie' and to the end of 'the old relations between masters and men' had already been set in motion by Smith.

Far from conceding that there might be more than one way of reading Smith, his 'gospel of industrial freedom', Ricardo's 'gold-seeking animals' and Charles Darwin's 'survival of the fittest' were treated as all of one piece. It was Smith's 'doctrine of freedom of labour' which became 'the principal weapon against the methods by which labourers have sought to improve their condition'. This doctrine, formalised by Ricardo and supplemented by Malthus's 'wage–fund theory' had produced the emergence of socialism in the work of two of Ricardo's disciples, Henry George and Karl Marx. Framing the antitheses in this way prepared the ground for Toynbee's solution, one of the first, but also one of the most influential of many proposals of 'a third way'.

Toynbee had established the outlines of a narrative which continued to dominate conceptions of the history of modern Britain throughout much of the twentieth century. It was qualified, but not fundamentally altered by debates between 'optimists' and 'pessimists' about the effect of the industrial revolution upon the standard of living of the working classes. On the left, historians were happy to endorse such an agenda, in part because it allowed Marx to intrude upon respectable historical debate, in part because of the conviction that the politics of the period concealed more basic and underlying social tensions. Typical of this approach was the belief of Mark Hovell, the first professional historian of Chartism, that Chartists could not have

thought that their aims would be realised by 'mere improvements of political machinery', that Chartism was therefore
'a protest against what existed ... a passionate negation'.
Edward Thompson challenged this assumption by placing
the politics of English Jacobinism centre stage in his *Making
of the English Working Class*, but returned to the Toynbee
tradition with his distinction between 'moral' and 'political'
economy, and in his refusal to draw significant distinctions
between the positions of Smith and Burke on the treatment
of scarcity.

On the centre left of British politics, Toynbee was even
more successful. Toynbee's approach captured perfectly
twentieth-century Labour's singular ability to combine
within one credo a commitment to socialise all means of
production, distribution and exchange, with an almost
Burkean respect for monarchical and aristocratic institutions. Socialism in England, it seemed, was not a form of
republicanism, but an alternative to it. Indeed, the only
groups left outside this broad consensus stretching from
church, landed classes and professionals to trade union-
ists, co-operators and communists, were businessmen, the
much-lampooned entrepreneurs and the sort of people the
early Mrs Thatcher respected – people of modest means
who saved, did not call upon the help of their neighbours
and kept themselves to themselves. It was not until the
1970s that historians drew attention to this imbalance and
began to attribute to it some responsibility for the decline of
Britain's 'industrial spirit'. But this insight was not pushed

far enough. Historical enquiry was largely confined to the Victorian period, and the question restricted to the impact of anti-industrialism upon economic performance. The creation of this anti-industrial mythology was not tracked back to its originating source.

∽

This book has been an argument for the relevance of history to the present, an attempt to demonstrate – especially in the history of ideas – that the long term matters. From the general argument, a number of more specific conclusions may be drawn.

One might concern the familiar claim that the ancestry of a radically individualist and libertarian position in economic affairs dates back to Adam Smith. This claim has already been subjected to extensive criticism elsewhere. What has been added here is a stronger emphasis upon what distinguished Smith from his successors in the 1790s, Burke and Malthus as much as Condorcet and Paine. Recent research has high-lighted Smith's fear of the doctrinaire approach of 'men of system': he had in mind in particular the French Physiocratic *economistes*. He placed considerable weight upon deference to the great and admiration of the rich, precisely because he considered that private property possessed such a shallow basis of legitimacy. But this form of timidity, or caution, had nothing in common with the Burkean relegation of the poor to an unquestioning acceptance of the views of the superior ranks in the social hierarchy or with the Malthusian equation of the mentality of the poor with the immediacy of the animal passions of fear or concupiscence.

Furthermore, by following the story beyond the 1790s, it becomes clearer how the notion of political economy as a simple and total gospel of economic or industrial freedom came into being. Although it is true that, even in 1800, contemporaries had ceased to make a distinction between Smith's views on scarcity and those of Burke or even Malthus, it was the writings of the Romantics – particularly Coleridge, Southey, Hazlitt and Carlyle – which seized upon this fleeting and largely mistaken assumption of identity and perpetuated it for posterity. Coleridge also made an attack on political economy's cosmopolitanism and its supposed apology for the labour of factory children; Southey on its association with the harshness of early Malthusian doctrine and the ugliness of the manufacturing town; Hazlitt and Peacock on the abstraction and pedantry of its language. Finally, distilling all these disparate forms of assault into one riveting image, Carlyle identified political economy with the reduction of all the qualitative richness and diversity of life to the emptiness of the 'cash nexus'.

When Toynbee sought to characterise the 'industrial revolution', he started out, not from the writings of Smith, but from this single and commanding image of Carlyle, whose paternity he then sought to transfer back to Smith. In the case of Smith, Toynbee's portrait is in large part caricature. But neo-conservatism has been happier with the caricature than a true likeness.

Another conclusion which might be drawn concerns the discursive character of the creation of 'class' in the early nineteenth century. The 1832 Reform Bill legislated the disfranchisement of existing working-class voters in scot and lot boroughs and the acquisition by the working classes of a specific political identity – that of *not* being represented in a new property-based representative political system. The process which led to this enactment dated back to the counter-revolutionary alarms of the 1790s. The so-called 'social interpretation' of the genesis of 'class' was not only false for the reasons to which I have alluded in a previous book, *Languages of Class*, in origin it was also part of the process by which the republican and democratic challenge to British politics in the 1790s was pushed into the background and replaced by another story, drawing upon the Romantics, Carlyle, a bit of Marx and Toynbee. Toynbee's account of the 'industrial revolution' insisted that it was the gospel of industrial freedom, not the French Revolution and its repression, which was responsible for the separation and alienation of classes. By diverting attention from the political reaction to the Revolution and resituating a period of trauma in a purely industrial or agrarian setting, the peculiarities of the British monarchical and constitutional system came to belong to the natural and the taken-for-granted.

The last and most important conclusion concerns the dating and nature of the beginnings of social democracy. Historians generally date its emergence to Bernstein's 'revisionist' critique of Marx in the 1890s, or the Fabians' substitution of Edgeworth's theory of rent in place of Marx's theory of capital. Others date social democracy to 1848 and Louis Blanc's proposals of a state socialism based upon partnership between producer associations and a Jacobin state authority. Others yet again point to the 1860s and the alleged deal struck up between Bismarck and Lassalle, the first leader of German social democracy, whose aim was to establish a form of state socialism.

But what the story told here suggests is that all these historical approaches put the cart before the horse. Social democracy *preceded* the genesis of nineteenth- or twentieth-century socialism, whether in its 'utopian' or 'scientific' form. The first thinkers and activists to build upon the works of Smith were libertarians of the left rather than of the right. However circumspect and politically cautious Adam Smith's own approach, readings of his work by the progressives of the 1780s and 1790s provided much of the foundation of a radical critique of aristocratic monopoly and the bellicose and inegalitarian state which protected it.

It was not Smith but the conservative reaction of the 1790s which produced the divorce between political economy and progressive politics. Indeed, it was precisely the ferocious reaction to what might be described as the first social democratic programme for the elimination of poverty and inequality that prompted the appearance of what came to be called 'socialism'. Socialism in the writings of Saint Simon, Fourier and Owen assumed a non-political and anti-republican form, not least to avoid the hostility encountered by

Condorcet, Paine and Godwin. Their 'utopian' or quasi-religious appearance helped to circumvent the formidable discursive and institutional obstacles, whether religious or political, erected by the enraged or demoralised regimes of the 1790s and 1800s.

The proposals of Condorcet and Paine derived from a unique juncture between the rationalist optimism of the Enlightenment, the impact of democratic revolutions and an exhilarating sense of the possibility of marrying Smith's conception of the potential of commercial society with a modern republican form. In the course of the nineteenth and twentieth centuries, this new language of citizenship was increasingly pushed aside by opposing extremes: on the one side, *laisser faire* individualism and a language of producer and consumer; on the other side, socialism and the language of worker and capitalist. Contemporary social democracy has too long attempted to navigate between these two extremes, both elaborated in the chilly and anti-political aftermath of the French Revolution. It should instead revisit its original birthplace and resume the ambition of the late and democratic Enlightenment to combine the benefits of individual freedom and commercial society with a republican ideal of greater equality, inclusive citizenship and the public good.

NOTES

Introduction

1 A. Smith, *The Theory of Moral Sentiments*, 12th edn (London, 1809), pt IV, ch. 1, pp. 248–9, 250.

2 See B. Hilton, *Corn, Cash, Commerce: The Economic Policies of the Tory Governments 1815–1830* (Oxford, 1977); on the conservative reception and recasting of Smith, see E. Rothschild, *Economic Sentiments: Smith, Condorcet and the Enlightenment* (Cambridge, Mass., 2001), ch. 2 & *passim*; on the broader religious and political framing of these changes, see B. Hilton, *The Age of Atonement: The Influence of Evangelicalism on Social and Economic Thought, 1795–1865* (Oxford, 1988); for its continuing impact upon government and charitable thinking in late Victorian England, see G. Stedman Jones, *Outcast London: A Study of the Relationship between Classes in Victorian Society* (Oxford, 1971).

3 On Hegel's conception of political economy and 'civil society', see G. Stedman Jones, 'Hegel and the Economics of Civil Society', in S. Kaviraj & S. Khilnani (eds.), *Civil Society: History and Possibilities* (Cambridge, 2001), pp. 105–31; on the combination of evangelical Christianity and possessive individualism in Vormärz Prussia and the part it played in the development of Young Hegelianism, see especially W.

Breckman, *Marx, the Young Hegelians, and the Origins of Radical Social Theory* (Cambridge, 1999).

4   Marx to Engels, 18 June 1862, Karl Marx & Frederick Engels, *Collected Works*, vol. 41 (London, 1985), p. 381.

5   See, for instance, F. A. Hayek, *Individualism and Economic Order* (Chicago, 1948); F. A. Hayek, *The Counter-Revolution of Science* (Illinois, 1952); G. Himmelfarb, *The Idea of Poverty: England in the Early Industrial Age* (London, 1984).

6   See J. De Vries, 'The Industrial Revolution and the Industrious Revolution', *Journal of Economic History* 54 (June 1994), no. 2, pp. 249–271.

7   J. Locke, *Two Treatises of Government*, P. Laslett (ed.), 14th edn (Cambridge, 2003), pp. 296–7; A. Smith, *An Inquiry into the Nature and Causes of the Wealth of Nations* (1776), E. Cannan (ed.) (Chicago, 1976), bk 1, ch. 1, p. 16. See the discussion of the significance in seventeenth- and eighteenth-century arguments about commercial society, in I. Hont, *Jealousy of Trade* (Cambridge, Mass., forthcoming), introduction.

8   T. Paine, *Rights of Man: Part Two* (1792), M. Conway (ed.), *The Writings of Thomas Paine*, 4 vols. (London, 1906), vol. 2, pp. 487–8.

9   A.-N. de Condorcet, *Sketch for a Historical Picture of the Progress of the Human Mind* (1795), J. Barraclough (trans.), S. Hampshire (ed.) (London, 1955), p. 180.

Chapter I

1   T. Paine, *Rights of Man: Part Two* (1792), M. Conway (ed.), *The Writings of Thomas Paine*, 4 vols. (London, 1906), vol. 2, p. 461.

2   A.-N. de Condorcet, *Sketch for a Historical Picture of the Progress of the Human Mind* (1795), J. Barraclough (trans.), S. Hampshire (ed.) (London, 1955), pp. 12, 169.

3   Condorcet, *Sketch*, pp. 173–4.

4   Condorcet, *Sketch*, pp. 176–7.

5   See R. Blackburn, *The Overthrow of Colonial Slavery 1776–1848*
     (London, 1988), p. 170.

6   Condorcet, *Sketch*, pp. 180–1.

7   Condorcet, *Sketch*, p. 181.

8   Condorcet, *Sketch*, p. 182; A.-N. de Condorcet, 'The Nature
     and Purpose of Public Instruction' (1791), K. M. Baker (ed.),
     Condorcet: Selected Writings (Indianapolis, 1976), p. 106.

9   As above, p. 126.

10   Paine, *Rights of Man: Part Two*, Conway, *The Writings of
     Thomas Paine*, vol. 2, p. 456.

11   Paine, *Rights of Man: Part One*, Conway, *The Writings of
     Thomas Paine*, vol. 2, pp. 316, 387; *Rights of Man: Part Two*,
     pp. 403, 438, 456, 485.

12   Paine, *Rights of Man: Part Two*, Conway, *The Writings of
     Thomas Paine*, vol. 2, pp. 476, 482–92; on the importance of
     Sinclair, see I. Hacking, *The Taming of Chance* (Cambridge,
     1990), pp. 26–8.

13   Paine, *Rights of Man: Part Two*, Conway, *The Writings of
     Thomas Paine*, vol. 2, pp. 501–2.

14   As above, pp. 501–2.

15   See A. O. Aldridge, 'Condorcet et Paine: leurs rapports
     intellectuels', *Revue de Littérature Comparée* 32 (1958), no.
     1, pp. 457–65; G. Kates, 'Tom Paine's *Rights of Man*', *Journal
     of the History of Ideas* (1958), pp. 569–87; W. Doyle, 'Tom
     Paine and the Girondins', in W. Doyle, *Officers, Nobles and
     Revolutionaries* (London, 1995), pp. 209–19; B. Vincent,
     'Thomas Paine républicain de l'univers', in F. Furet & M.
     Ozouf (eds.), *Le Siècle de l'avènement republicain* (Paris, 1993),
     pp. 101–26; J. P. Lagrave, 'Thomas Paine et les Condorcet', in B.
     Vincent (ed.), *Thomas Paine ou la République sans frontières*
     (Nancy, 1993), pp. 57–65; G. Claeys, *Thomas Paine: Social and
     Political Thought* (London, 1989), ch. 4; see also A. O. Aldridge,

Man of Reason: The Life of Thomas Paine (London, 1959); J. Keane, *Tom Paine: A Political Life* (London, 1995).

16 Condorcet, 'Reception Speech at the French Academy' (1782), in Baker, *Condorcet: Selected Writings*, p. 6; the best account of what Condorcet meant by 'the calculus of probabilities' is to be found in K. M. Baker, *Condorcet: From Natural Philosophy to Social Mathematics* (Chicago, 1975); see also L. Daston, *Classical Probability in the Enlightenment* (Princeton, 1988), esp. pp. 210–25; Hacking, *The Taming of Chance*, ch. 5.

17 Condorcet, *Sketch*, p. 162.

18 As above, pp. 162, 181.

19 Paine, *Rights of Man: Part Two*, Conway, *The Writings of Thomas Paine*, vol. 2, pp. 488–9.

20 T. Paine, *Agrarian Justice* (1797), M. Conway (ed.), *The Writings of Thomas Paine*, 4 vols. (London, 1906), vol. 3, pp. 333, 337.

21 See Daston, *Classical Probability in the Enlightenment*, pp. 27–30, 127–9.

22 On Leibniz's memoir, see Hacking, *The Taming of Chance*, pp. 18–20.

23 On the significance of changes in eighteenth-century attitudes towards insurance and the importance of The Society for Equitable Insurance, see L. Daston, 'The Domestication of Risk: Mathematical Probability and Insurance, 1650–1830', in L. Kruger, L. J. Daston & M. Heidelberger (eds.) *The Probabilistic Revolution*, vol. 1, *Ideas in History* (Cambridge, Mass., 1987), pp. 237–61. But see also G. Clark, *Betting on Lives, The Culture of Life Insurance in England, 1695–1775* (Manchester, 1999), esp. pp. 117–18, where resistance to a statistical approach to death is ascribed, not to the absence of a prudential attitude towards insurance before 1750, but to the persistence of popular and often credible beliefs about mortality patterns.

24 Cited in Daston, 'The Domestication of Risk', p. 250.

25 See Baker, *Condorcet: From Natural Philosophy to Social Mathematics*, pp. 279–82; Hacking, *The Taming of Chance*, pp. 44–6.

26 See J.-A.-N. Caritat Marquis de Condorcet, *Vie de Monsieur Turgot* (1783) (Paris, 1997), p. 187; A. R. J. Turgot, 'A Philosophical Review of the Successive Advances of the Human Mind', in R. L. Meek (ed.), *Turgot on Progress, Sociology and Economics* (Cambridge, 1973), pp. 41–59; Baker, *Condorcet: From Natural Philosophy to Social Mathematics*, p. 207.

27 Cited in D. Winch, *Riches and Poverty: An Intellectual History of Political Economy in Britain 1750–1834* (Cambridge, 1996), p. 90. Winch's book is an invaluable source on the contrary uses made of Smith's work in the two generations following his death.

28 A. Smith, *The Theory of Moral Sentiments*, 12th edn (London, 1809), pt IV, ch. 1, p. 10.

29 R. L. Meek, D. D. Raphael & P. G. Stein (eds.), A. Smith, *Lectures on Jurisprudence* (Oxford, 1976), p. 208; on Smith's fears of the systematic plans of reform associated with the *economistes*, see I. Hont, 'The Political Economy of the "Unnatural and Retrograde" Order: Adam Smith and Natural Liberty', in *Französische Revolution und politische ökonomie*, Karl-Marx-Haus Trier (1989), pp. 122–49.

30 Paine, *Agrarian Justice*, Conway, *The Writings of Thomas Paine*, vol. 3, p. 341.

31 Condorcet, *Vie de Monsieur Turgot*, p. 164; Condorcet, *Sketch*, pp. 127, 163.

32 In this context, the link between between Turgot, Condorcet and Smith derives as much from Smith's *Theory of Moral Sentiments* as from *The Wealth of Nations*. In each there is a new emphasis upon the reflective character of human beings and an aversion to mechanical and determinist theories. These linkages are powerfully brought to the fore in E.

Rothschild, *Economic Sentiments: Adam Smith, Condorcet and the Enlightenment* (Cambridge, Mass., 2001), esp. ch. 8 & *passim*. Particularly important was a shared idea of 'economic enlightenment' linked to a dynamic view of history and cultural/mental development, as against static and ahistorical conceptions of self-interest. See, for example, the distaste for Helvetius manifested in the correspondence between Turgot and Condorcet. Rothschild, *Economic Sentiments*, pp. 199–201.

33 Dugald Stewart, 'Account of the Life and Writings of Adam Smith', I. S. Ross (ed.), in W. P. D. Wightman & J. C. Bryce, *Adam Smith: Essays on Philosophical Subjects* (Oxford, 1980), p. 304.

34 Condorcet, *Sketch*, p. 180; he had already addressed this theme more explicitly in his *Essai sur les assemblées provinciales* of 1788, where he argued that the first cause of poverty was the unequal distribution of wealth due to bad laws and that the second was low wages due to the obstruction of free competition caused by guild and apprenticeship regulation, A.Condorcet O'Connor & M. F. Arago (eds.), *Oeuvres de Condorcet*, 12 vols. (Paris 1847–9), vol. 8, pp. 453–9; and see Rothschild, *Economic Sentiments*, pp. 171–2; see also L. Cahen, *Condorcet et la révolution française* (Paris, 1904), pp. 83–7.

35 Baker, *Condorcet: From Natural Philosophy to Social Mathematics*, p. 208.

36 Condorcet, 'The Nature and Purpose of Public Instruction', in Baker, *Condorcet: Selected Writings*, p. 106.

37 As above, p. 119.

38 See Condorcet, *Vie de Monsieur Turgot*, p. 171.

39 Baker, *Condorcet: From Natural Philosophy to Social Mathematics*, pp. 292–3.

40 Paine, *Rights of Man: Part One*, Conway, *The Writings of Thomas Paine*, vol. 2, p. 314; *Rights of Man: Part Two*, Conway, *The Writings of Thomas Paine*, vol. 2, p. 413.

41   E. Canaan (ed.), Adam Smith, *An Enquiry into the Nature and Causes of the Wealth of Nations* (1776) (Chicago, 1976), bk 3, ch. 2, p. 409.

42   Paine, *Agrarian Justice*, Conway, *The Writings of Thomas Paine*, vol. 3, pp. 328, 330. The different inferences writers around the time of the French Revolution drew from the so-called 'agrarian law' was of central importance in determining divergent paths of radicalism in the nineteenth century. See G. Stedman Jones, 'Introduction', in G. Stedman Jones (ed.), *Karl Marx and Friedrich Engels: The Communist Manifesto* (London, 2002), pp. 149–55.

43   Condorcet, *Sketch*, p. 32.

44   Condorcet, 'The Nature and Purpose of Public Instruction', Baker, *Condorcet: Selected Writings*, p. 109; *Sketch*, pp. 180, 192.

45   Paine, *Rights of Man: Part Two*, Conway, *The Writings of Thomas Paine*, vol. 2, pp. 409, 456; *Agrarian Justice*, Conway, *The Writings of Thomas Paine*, vol. 3, p. 337; *Rights of Man: Part Two*, Conway, *The Writings of Thomas Paine*, vol. 2, p. 496.

46   See I. Hont, 'Commerce and Luxury', in M. Goldie & R. Wokler (eds.), *The Cambridge History of Eighteenth-century Political Thought* (forthcoming), ch. 14; see also E. J. Hundert, *The Enlightenment's Fable: Bernard Mandeville and the Discovery of Society* (Cambridge, 1994); P. Riley (ed.), F. de Fénelon, *Telemachus, Son of Ulysses* (Cambridge, 1994).

47   I. Kramnick (ed.), William Godwin, *Enquiry Concerning Political Justice* (1798) (Harmondsworth, 1976), p. 171.

48   See Winch, *Riches and Poverty*, ch. 3; Rothschild, *Economic Sentiments*, pp. 68–71.

49   See Winch, *Riches and Poverty*, pp. 76–80.

50   See D. O. Thomas, *The Honest Mind: The Thought and Work of Richard Price* (Oxford, 1977), p. 230.

51   Smith, *The Theory of Moral Sentiments*, pt. iv, ch. 1, p. 10.

52   R. Price, 'A Future Period of Improvement'(1787) in D. O. Thomas (ed.), Richard Price, *Political Writings* (Cambridge, 1991), pp. 164, 165; on the relationship between the American Revolution and British radical dissent, see P. N. Miller, *Defining the Common Good: Empire, Religion and Philosophy in Eighteenth-century Britain* (Cambridge, 1994); on the character of British radicalism in the 1780s and its reaction to the first years of the French Revolution, see R. Whatmore, 'A Gigantic Manliness: Paine's Republicanism in the 1790s', in S. Collini, R. Whatmore & B. Young (eds.), *Economy, Polity, and Society: British Intellectual History 1750–1950* (Cambridge, 2000), pp. 141–6. On the salience of calls for moral reform in the 1780s, see J. Innes, 'Politics and Morals: The Reformation of Manners Movement in Later Eighteenth-century England', in E. Hellmuth (ed.), *The Transformation of Political Culture: England and Germany in the Later Eighteenth Century* (Oxford, 1990), pp. 57–119.

53   See F. Acomb, *Anglophobia in France (1763–89)* (Durham, NC, 1950) and Whatmore, 'A Gigantic Manliness' in Collini *et al.*, *Economy, Polity, and Society*, pp. 148–9.

54   A.-N. Condorcet, 'On the Influence of the American Revolution in Europe' (1786), Baker, *Condorcet: Selected Writings*, p. 81.

55   For Paine's American experience and its impact upon his thought, see E. Foner, *Tom Paine and Revolutionary America* (New York, 1976), chs. 3, 4, 6 & *passim*.

56   Whatmore, 'A Gigantic Manliness' in Collini *et al. Economy, Polity, and Society*, pp. 135–58; see also A. O. Aldridge, *Franklin and His French Contemporaries* (New York, 1957).

57   Paine, *Rights of Man: Part One*, Conway, *The Writings of Thomas Paine*, vol. 2, p. 383; *Rights of Man: Part Two*, Conway, *The Writings of Thomas Paine*, vol. 2, p. 437.

58   Paine, *Rights of Man: Part Two*, Conway, *The Writings of Thomas Paine*, vol. 2, pp. 403–4, 471; *Rights of Man: Part One*, Conway, *The Writings of Thomas Paine*, vol. 2, p. 321.

59   T. Paine, *Common Sense*, (1776), Conway, *The Writings of Thomas Paine*, vol. 1, p. 83.

60   Condorcet, *Vie de Monsieur Turgot*, pp. 173–5; 'On the Influence of the American Revolution on Europe', Baker, *Condorcet: Selected Writings*, p. 74.

61   'The Explanatory Note of M. Sieyès in Answer to the Letter of Mr Paine, and to Several Other Provocations of the Same Sort', in M. Sonenscher (ed.), Sieyès, *Political Writings* (Indianapolis, 2003), pp. 169–73; and on the basis of Sieyès' position, see the introduction and notes, pp. vii–lxiv, 163–4.

62   Paine, *Rights of Man: Part Two*, Conway, *The Writings of Thomas Paine*, vol. 2, ch. 3, p. 422.

63   Paine, *Rights of Man: Part Two*, Conway, *The Writings of Thomas Paine*, vol. 2, pp. 406, 414.

64   Smith, *The Wealth of Nations*, bk. 1, ch. 1, p. 16; Paine, *Rights of Man: Part Two*, Conway, *The Writings of Thomas Paine*, vol. 2, p. 454.

65   Paine, *Rights of Man: Part Two*, Conway, *The Writings of Thomas Paine*, vol. 2, pp. 415–16, 422–4.

66   As above, p. 498.

67   Paine, *Agrarian Justice*, Conway, *The Writings of Thomas Paine*, vol. 3, p. 325; *Rights of Man: Part Two*, Conway, *The Writings of Thomas Paine*, vol. 2, p. 495.

68   Cited in I. Woloch, *The New Regime: Transformations of the French Civic Order, 1789–1820s* (New York, 1994), p. 244.

69   Paine, *Rights of Man: Part Two*, Conway, *The Writings of Thomas Paine*, vol. 2, pp. 456, 512.

70   Although she has an interesting interpretation of Paine, I cannot agree with Gertrude Himmelfarb that Paine's position was just another proposal for Poor Law reform.

Himmelfarb makes no reference to the fact that Paine was primarily attempting to intervene in a debate in France. See G. Himmelfarb, *The Idea of Poverty: England in the Early Industrial Age* (London, 1984), pp. 86–99.

Chapter II

1   Cited in E. P. Thompson, *The Making of the English Working Class* (London, 1963), p. 112.

2   See N. Rogers, *Crowds, Culture and Politics in Georgian Britain* (Oxford, 1998), pp. 197, 203 & ch. 6 *passim*.

3   R. A. & S. Wilberforce, *The Life of William Wilberforce*, 5 vols. (London, 1838), vol. 2, pp. 3–5.

4   R. Price, 'A Discourse on the Love of Our Country', *Political Writings* (Cambridge, 1991), pp. 190, 195.

5   E. Burke, *Reflections on the Revolution in France and on the Proceedings in Certain Societies in London Relative to That Event* (1790) (Harmondsworth, 1968), pp. 157–9. Price in the same passage had referred to 'their king led in triumph, and an arbitrary monarch surrendering himself to his subjects'. Burke took this as a reference to the events of October 5–6 1789, when the people of Paris forced the Royal Family to return from Versailles to the Tuileries. Price called this a 'horrid misrepresentation' and said that his remarks referred to the fall of the Bastille on 14 July and the king's showing himself to his people as the restorer of their liberty. See Price, *Political Writings*, pp. 176–7.

6   Cited in Thompson, *The Making of the English Working Class*, p. 110.

7   Cited in Rogers, *Crowds, Culture and Politics*, p. 207; see also J. Barrell, *Imagining the King's Death: Figurative Treason, Fantasies of Regicide 1793–1796* (Oxford, 2000).

8   See especially E. Rothschild, 'Adam Smith and Conservative
     Economics', *Economic History Review* 45 (Feb. 1992), pp. 74–96.

9   (T. R. Malthus), *First Essay on Population 1798* (London, 1966),
     pp. 303–4.

10 D. Stewart, 'Account of the Life and Writings of Adam Smith,
     LLD', in I. Ross (ed.), *Adam Smith Essays on Philosophical
     Subjects* (Oxford, 1980), p. 311.

11 According to McCulloch, Dugald Stewart omitted to mention
     that when Smith was a student at Oxford he was reprimanded
     by the university authorities for possessing and reading
     Hume's *Treatise of Human Nature*. J. R. McCulloch (ed.), *An
     Inquiry into the Nature and Causes of the Wealth of Nations
     by Adam Smith LLD; with a Life of the Author* (1838), 4th edn
     (Edinburgh, 1850), p. ii.

12 E. Burke, 'Preface to the Address of M. Brissot to His
     Constituents', *The Works of the Right Honourable Edmund
     Burke*, 8 vols. (London, 1803), vol. 7, p. 299. Burke was
     incensed that the education of the Dauphin had been passed
     to Condorcet, and that he had therefore been handed over
     'to this fanatick atheist, and furious democratic republican'.
     E. Burke, 'Thoughts on French Affairs', *The Works of the Right
     Honourable Edmund Burke*, vol. 7, p. 58.

13 See E. Rothschild, 'Adam Smith and Conservative Economics',
     p. 80. The effort to blot out the ideas of Condorcet appears
     to have been very successful. A single edition of an English
     translation of Condorcet's *Sketch* appeared in 1795, but was not
     republished until a new translation appeared in 1955.

14 G. Claeys, 'The French Revolution Debate and British Political
     Thought', *History of Political Thought* 11, 1 (Spring 1990),
     pp. 59–80; see also I. Hampsher-Monk, 'John Thelwell and
     the eighteenth century radical response to political economy',
     Historical Journal, 34, 1 (1991), pp. 1–20.

15 For Smith's argument, see Smith, *The Wealth of Nations*, bk 3, ch. 2, pp. 407–9.

16 For background, see J. R. Poynter, *Society and Pauperism, English Ideas on Poor Relief, 1795–1834* (London, 1969), chs. 1, 2 & *passim*; J. Innes, 'The Distinctiveness of the English Poor Laws, 1750–1850', in D. Winch & P. K. O'Brien(eds.), *The Political Economy of British Historical Experience 1688–1914* (Oxford, 2002), pp. 381–409; T. Horne, *Property Rights and Poverty: Political Argument in Britain 1605–1834* (Exeter, 1986).

17 T. Ruggles, *The History of the Poor, Their Rights, Duties and the Laws Respecting Them*, 2 vols. (London, 1793), vol. 1, pp. xv, 10. See also P. Slack, *Poverty and Policy in Tudor and Stuart England* (London, 1988).

18 See Innes, 'The Distinctiveness of the English Poor Laws', pp. 385–91.

19 N. Scarfe (ed.), *A Frenchman's Year in Suffolk: French Impressions of Suffolk Life in 1784* (Woodbridge, 1988), p. 215; see also F. Dreyfus, *La Rochefoucauld-Liancourt 1747–1827, un Philanthrope d'autrefois* (Paris, 1903), pp. 14–15.

20 F. M. Eden, *The State of the Poor*, 3 vols. (London, 1797), vol. 3, p. cccxi.

21 See Eden, *The State of the Poor*, appendix xi & see also G. Himmelfarb, *The Idea of Poverty: England in the Early Industrial Age* (London, 1984), pp. 73–8.

22 T. Paine, *Agrarian Justice (1797)*, M. Conway (ed.), *The Writings of Thomas Paine*, 4 vols. (London, 1906), vol. 3, pp. 338–9.

23 Burke, *Reflections*, pp. 256, 262.

24 See R. Hole, *Pulpits, Politics and Public Order in England, 1760–1832* (Cambridge, 1989), p. 102, and for an excellent overview part II *passim*.

25 Paine, *Rights of Man: Part Two*, Conway, *The Writings of Thomas Paine*, vol. 2, p. 514.

26   M. Wollstonecraft, *An Historical and Moral View of the Origin and Progress of the French Revolution* (London, 1794), vol. 1, pp. 21–2; for Wollstonecraft's own religious views, see B. Taylor, *Mary Wollstonecraft and the Feminist Imagination* (Cambridge, 2003), ch. 3.

27   H. More, 'The History of Mr Fantom, the New-fashioned Philosopher', *The Works of Hannah More*, 11 vols. (London, 1830), vol. 3, p. 12.

28   Wollstonecraft, *An Historical and Moral View of the French Revolution*, pp. 234–5.

29   On the centrality of the presence of the poor as an object of compassion and contemplation in the world of early Christianity in contrast to its insignificance in the outlook of pagan antiquity, see P. Brown, 'Late Antiquity', in P. Veyne, *A History of Private Life*, vol. 1, *From Pagan Rome to Byzantium* (Cambridge, Mass., 1987), pp. 235–97.

30   W. Wilberforce, *A Practical View of the Prevailing Religious System of Professed Christians in the Higher and Middle Classes in This Country Contrasted with Real Christianity* (London, 1797), pp. 404–5.

31   H. More, 'Strictures on the Modern System of Female Education; with a View of the Principles and Conduct Prevalent among Women of Rank and Fortune', *The Works of Hannah More*, vol. 5, p. 25.

32   Wilberforce, *A Practical View of the Prevailing Religious System*, p. 405.

33   More, 'The History of Mr Fantom', *The Works of Hannah More*, vol. 3, pp. 28–9.

34   Burke, *Reflections*, pp. 211, 265; 'Thoughts on French Affairs' (1791), *The Works of the Right Honourable Edmund Burke*, vol. 7, pp. 13, 49, 57, 58; 'Three Letters Addressed to a Member of the Present Parliament, on Proposals for Peace with the

Regicide Directory of France' (1796), *The Works of the Right Honourable Edmund* Burke, vol. 8, pp. 98, 169, 236, 259.

35 J. Mackintosh, *Vindiciae Gallicae, Defence of the French Revolution and Its English Admirers against the Accusations of the Right Honourable Edmund Burke*, 3rd edn (London, 1791), pp. 140–1. The detachment of radicals from Christianity, in Britain at least, appears to have been more an effect than a cause of support for the Revolution. See M. Butler, *Romantics, Rebels & Reactionaries: English Literature and Background 1760–1830* (Oxford, 1981), esp. ch. 3.

36 J. Robison, *Proofs of a Conspiracy against All the Religions and Governments of Europe*, 2nd edn (London, 1797), pp. 374–5; see also A. de Barruel, *Memoirs Illustrating the History of Jacobinism: A Translation* (London, 1797).

37 T. Paine, *The Age of Reason*, ch. 1 'The Author's Profession of Faith', Conway, *The Writings of Thomas Paine*, vol. 4, p. 21.

38 E. Burke, 'Letters on a Regicide Peace', *The Works of the Right Honourable Edmund Burke*, vol. 7, pp. 368–9.

39 E. Burke, 'Thoughts and Details on Scarcity', *The Works of the Right Honourable Edmund Burke*, vol. 7, pp. 376, 377, 386, 391, 404.

40 See Rothschild, 'Smith and Conservative Economics', p. 87; and see also D. Winch, *Riches and Poverty: An Intellectual History of Political Economy in Britain, 1750–1834* (Cambridge, 1996), ch. 8. For an account of how the problem of scarcities and famines was approached by Turgot and Smith, see Rothschild, *Economic Sentiments*, ch. 3; and see also S. L. Kaplan, *Bread, Politics and Political Economy in the Reign of Louis XV* (The Hague, 1976).

41 (T. R. Malthus), *An Essay on the Principle of Population as It Affects the Future Improvement of Society with Remarks on the Speculations of Mr Godwin, M. Condorcet, and Other Writers* (London, 1798), p. 17.

42   In March 1793, in an appendix to a pamphlet, *Peace and
      Union Recommended*, Frend contrasted the wartime plight
      of poor country women near the Cambridgeshire village of
      St Ives whose earnings were 'to be scotched three pence in
      the shilling' with that of rich war profiteers whose incomes
      alone should have been 'scotched' by a quarter to pay for the
      war and relieve the plight of its poverty-stricken victims. For
      this, he was expelled from his college fellowship at Queen's
      College and ejected from the university. Frend had also been
      Coleridge's tutor while at Cambridge. See A. Goodwin, *The
      Friends of Liberty: The English Democratic Movement in the
      Age of the French Revolution* (London, 1979), pp. 268–9. On the
      connections between socinianism (the denial of the Trinity)
      and political radicalism before the French Revolution, see J. C.
      D. Clark, *English Society, 1688–1832: Ideology, Social Structure
      and Political Practice during the Ancien Régime* (Cambridge,
      1985), pp. 330–46.

43   On Malthus's politics, see especially Winch, *Riches and
      Poverty*, pt III; and see also P. James, *Population Malthus*
      (London, 1979). After 1815, although he was still in principle
      a Whig, his politics became increasingly conservative. His
      semi-Physiocratic views on agriculture led him to defend
      landlords and support the Corn Laws, while his distrust of
      manufacturing and towns made him increasingly fearful of
      crowds and popular disturbance.

44   For an account of the theology and theological context of
      Malthus's *Essay*, see especially A. M. C. Waterman, *Revolution,
      Economics and Religion: Christian Political Economy, 1798–1833*
      (Cambridge, 1991), chs. 3 & 4; see also D. L. Le Mahieu,
      'Malthus and the Theology of Scarcity', *Journal of the History of
      Ideas* 40, pp. 467–74.

45   D. Stewart, 'Critical Examination of a Late *Essay on the
      Principle of Population as It Affects the Future Improvement of*

Society', 'Plan of Lectures on Political Economy for the Winter 1800–1', *The Collected Works of Dugald Stewart, Esq. FRSS*, W. Hamilton (ed.), 11 vols. (Edinburgh, 1855), vol. 8, p. 203; and discussed in Waterman, *Revolution, Economics and Religion*, pp. 113–14. On the impact of Stewart on the positions adopted by the *Edinburgh Review*, see B. Fontana, *Rethinking the Politics of Commercial Society* (Cambridge, 1983).

46 For an account of the development of natural theology in eighteenth-century Cambridge, see Waterman, *Revolution, Economics and Religion*, ch. 3.

47 I. Kramnick (ed.), William Godwin, *Enquiry Concerning Political Justice* (1798) (Harmondsworth, 1976), pp. 751–2, 759, 763.

48 (Malthus), *An Essay*, pp. 286–7, 351, 358.

49 (Malthus), *An Essay*, pp. 353, 354, 357, 363.

50 (Malthus), *An Essay*, pp. 11, 353, 364, 365, 369, 395.

51 (Malthus), *An Essay*, pp. 176–7.

52 (Malthus), *An Essay*, pp. 148–50.

53 Smith, *The Wealth of Nations*, bk 1, pp. 81–2, 91; bk 5, p. 321.

54 On this topic, see E. Rothschild, 'Social Security and Laissez Faire in Eighteenth-century Political Economy', *Population and Economic Development* 21, (Dec. 1995), pp. 711–44.

55 Smith, *The Wealth of Nations*, bk 1, pp. 19–20; *The Theory of Moral Sentiments*, 12th edn (Glasgow, 1809), pt I, sect 3, ch. 2, p. 86.

56 (Malthus), *An Essay*, pp. 86–7, 88, 254.

57 Malthus's theological deficiencies are discussed in Waterman, *Revolution, Economics and Religion*, pp. 106–12.

58 Waterman, *Revolution, Economics and Religion*, pp. 142–4.

59 Although it should not be forgotten that Malthus has never lacked influential advocates. See especially the admiring study by Keynes in 'Essay in Biography', in E. Johnson and D.

Moggridge, *The Collected Writings of John Maynard Keynes*, 29 vols. (London, 1971–82), vol. 10.

60   (Malthus), *An Essay*, pp. 32–3.

61   E. A. Wrigley, 'Malthus on the Labouring Poor', in E. A. Wrigley (ed.), *Poverty, Progress and Population* (Cambridge, 2004), pp. 243, 244–5.

62   See P. H. Marshall, *William Godwin* (Yale, 1984), ch. 10; Winch, *Riches and Poverty*, p. 305.

63   Condorcet, *Sketch*, pp. 188–9; for Condorcet's unpublished larger manuscript on the subject, see I. Cahen, 'Condorcet inédit. Notes pour le tableau des progrès de l'esprit humain', *La Revolution française* 75 (1922), pp. 193–212; (Malthus), *An Essay*, pp. 153–4; Godwin, *Enquiry*, pp. 767–70; Winch, *Riches and Poverty*, pp. 305–6. On the idea of 'promiscuous concubinage' as a cause of sterility, see J. Spengler, *French Predecessors of Malthus* (Durham, NC, 1942); T. Laquer in M. Feher (ed.), *Fragments for a History of the Human Body* (New York, 1989), pt III, p. 339; B. Wilson, 'Charles Fourier (1772–1837) and Questions of Women', PhD thesis, Cambridge, 2002.

64   Winch, *Riches and Poverty*, p. 314; for an argument contrary to Malthus that the enhanced sense of security afforded by Poor Laws assisted the mobility of labour in early modern England, see R. M. Smith, 'Transfer Incomes, Risk and Security: The Roles of the Family and the Collectivity in Recent Theories of Fertility Change', in D. Coleman & R. Schofield (eds.), *The State of Population Theory: Forward from Malthus* (Oxford, 1986).

65   T. R. Malthus, *An Essay on the Principle of Population or a View of Its Past and Present Effects on Human Happiness* (1803), 2 vols., P. James (ed.) (Cambridge, 1989), vol. 2, pp. 122, 123, 126.

66   Malthus, *An Essay*, 1803 edn, p. 127.

67   Malthus, *An Essay*, 1803 edn, p. 127.

68 M. Philp, 'English Republicanism in the 1790s', *Journal of Political Philosophy* 6, 3 (1998), pp. 235–62.

69 See L. Colley, 'The Apotheosis of George III: Loyalty, Royalty and the British Nation 1760–1820', *Past and Present* 102 (1984), pp. 94–129; P. Spence, *The Birth of Romantic Radicalism* (Aldershot, 1996).

70 Malthus, *An Essay*, 1803 edn, pp. 123–4.

71 G. Claeys, 'The French Revolution Debate and British Political Thought', *History of Political Thought* 11, no. 1 (Spring 1990), pp. 59–80; on the ultra radicals, see I. McCalman, *Radical Underworld: Prophets, Revolutionaries and Pornographers in London, 1795–1840* (Oxford, 1993).

72 (Malthus), *An Essay*, p. 85.

73 In 1817, Malthus wrote in support of savings banks which, 'as far as they go, appear to me much the best, and the most likely, if they should become general, to effect a permanent improvement in the condition of the lower classes of society'. But he stressed that this could only be a partial remedy and strongly opposed any parish assistance in the establishment and administration of such funds. See Malthus, *An Essay*, 1817 edn, vol. 3, 275; see also pp. 277–8.

74 J. S. Mill, 'The Claims of Labour', cited in Winch, *Riches and Poverty*, p. 405.

75 (Malthus), *An Essay*, p. 287.

76 J. B. Sumner, *A Treatise on the Records of Creation; with Particular Reference to the Jewish History, and the Consistency of the Principle of Population with the Wisdom and Goodness of the Deity*, 2 vols. (London, 1816), vol. 2, pp. 7, 8, 14, 25; and see the discussion of Sumner in Waterman, *Revolution, Economics and Religion*, pp. 160–3. Sumner was also a member of the royal commission whose report led to the Poor Law Amendment Act of 1834. There is unfortunately no space to discuss here how the campaign to abolish the Poor Law concluded by

amending the act. Malthus himself thought that the abolition of the Poor Law ought to be a gradual process. There has been a long discussion among historians about the intellectual and political authorship of the act. For a general account, see J. R. Poynter, *Society and Pauperism: English Ideas on Poor Relief, 1795–1834* (London, 1969).

Chapter III

1   J. B. Say, 'Discours préliminaire', *Traité d'économie politique ou simple exposition de la manière dont se forment, se distribuent et se consomment les richesses*, 2 vols. (Paris, 1803), vol. 1, pp. i–iv, xx–xxi. On Smith, Say wrote, 'but between his doctrine and that of the economists, there is the same distance which separates the system of *Ticho-Brahe* from the physics of Newton; before Smith, some true principles had been put forward several times; but he is the first to show the true connection between them, and how they arise as necessary consequences of the nature of things.' As above, pp. xx–xxi, and see p. xliv.

2   See G.Lefèbvre, *The Coming of the French Revolution* (New York, 1947); C. Bloch, *L'Assistance et l'état en France à la veille de la Revolution* (Paris, 1908), bk 3, pp. 361–550; F. Dreyfus, *Un philanthrope d'autrefois, La Rochefoucauld-Liancourt 1747–1827* (Paris, 1903), pp. 138–200.

3   See O. Hufton, *The Poor of Eighteenth-century France 1750–1789* (Oxford, 1974), pt II & *passim*; A. Forrest, *The French Revolution and the Poor* (Oxford, 1981), ch. 1.

4   Forrest, *The French Revolution and the Poor*, pp. 27–8; I. Woloch, *The New Regime: Transformations of the French Civic Order, 1789–1820s* (New York, 1994), pp. 244–5 & chs. 8 & 9.

5   Bloch, *L'Assistance et l'état*, p. 443.

6   See Hufton, *The Poor of Eighteenth-century France*, chs. 2 &
    12; Woloch, *The New Regime*, pp. 244–8; Bloch, *L'Assistance et
    l'état*, pp. 436–42.

7   Cited in C. Jones, *The Great Nation: France from Louis XV to
    Napoleon 1715–99* (London, 2002), p. 494.

8   Forrest, *The French Revolution and the Poor*, p. 172.

9   Woloch, *The New Regime*, pp. 254–8.

10 J. B. Say, *Olbie ou essai sur les moyens de reformer les moeurs
    d'une nation* (Paris, yr 8 (1800)), p. 3.

11 On Say's early career and his relationship with Clavière, see
    R. Whatmore, *Republicanism and the French Revolution: An
    Intellectual History of Jean-Baptiste Say's Political Economy*
    (Oxford, 2000), chs. 3–6.

12 R. Price, 'Observations on the Importance of the American
    Revolution and the Means of Making it a Benefit to the World',
    in D. O. Thomas (ed.), R. Price, *Political Writings* (Cambridge,
    1991), p. 119.

13 As above, pp. 145–6.

14 Asked what he did during the Terror, the Abbé Sieyès
    answered, 'J'ai vécu' ('I lived').

15 B. Franklin, *Poor Richard: The Almanacks for the Years 1733–1758
    by Richard Saunders* (Philadelphia, 1976), p.278.

16 Cited in Whatmore, *Republicanism and the French Revolution*,
    p. 117.

17 Say, *Olbie*, pp. 23–5.

18 Say, *Olbie*, pp. 23, 29, 33–4, 42–3.

19 Say, *Olbie*, pp. 12–15, 19.

20 Say, *Olbie*, pp. 3–5, 85–6, 91–4, 102; for Fourier's mockery of the
    Christian heaven, see G. Stedman Jones (ed.), C. Fourier, *The
    Theory of the Four Movements* (Cambridge, 1996), pp. 200–1.

21 Say, *Olbie*, pp. 1, 8.

22 Say, *Olbie*, pp. 5, 27, 48–9, 71, 75.

23 Say, *Olbie*, pp. 29–31, 106.

24 Say, 'Discours préliminaire', *Traité d'économie politique* (1803), vol. 1, p. xliii; he expanded these remarks in the second edition of 1814, see 'Discours préliminaire', *Traité d'économie politique*, vol. 1, p. xcii; vol. 3, pp. 52, 56, 61, 174.

25 The Physiocratic political economist Dupont de Nemours attacked him for deferring to English ideas. He begged him to 'leave the counting house' and return to the French language of liberty. Cited in Whatmore, *Republicanism and the French Revolution*, p. 38.

26 Say, 'Discours préliminaire', *Traité d'économie politique* (1814), vol. 1, p. xcv.

27 Say, *Traité d'économie politique*, vol. 2, p. 288.

28 I develop this argument in *Before God Died: The Rise and Fall of the Socialist Utopia* (forthcoming).

Chapter IV

1   See M. Berg, *The Machinery Question and the Making of Political Economy, 1815–1848* (Cambridge, 1980); for a general survey see M. I. Thomis, *Responses to Industrialisation* (Newton Abbot, 1976); G. Claeys, *Machinery, Money and the Millennium* (Cambridge, 1987).

2   The relevant discussion in Smith is found in *The Wealth of Nations*, vol. 1, bk 2, ch. 5, pp. 384–5.

3   H. Gouhier, *La Jeunesse d'Auguste Comte et la formation de positivisme* (Paris, 1970), pt III, ch. 2; E. Alix, 'J. B. Say et les origines de l'industrialisme?', *Revue d'économie politique* (1910). P. Steiner, 'Politique et l'économie politique chez Jean-Baptiste Say', *Revue française d'histoire des idées politiques* 5 (1997), pp. 23–58. See S. M. Gruner, 'Political historiography in Restoration France', *History and Theory* (1972), pp. 346–65; M. James, 'Pierre-Louis Roederer, Jean Baptiste Say and the Concept of *industrie*', *History of Political Economy* 9 (1977), pp. 455–75; T. Kaiser, 'Politics and Political Economy in the Thought of the

Idéologues', *History of Political Economy* 12 (1980), pp. 142–59;
C. B. Welch, *Liberty and Utility. The French Idéologues and the
Transformation of Liberalism* (New York, 1984), ch. 3.

4 E. J. Sièyes, 'What is the Third Estate?', M. Sonenscher (ed.),
Sieyès, *Political Writings* (Indianapolis, 2003), pp. 92–163.

5 J. B. Say, *Traité d'économie politique, ou simple exposition de
la manière dont se forment, se distribuent et se consomment les
richesses* (Paris, 1814), vol. 1, pp. 40–52. See P. Steiner, 'La Théorie
de la Production de Jean-Baptiste Say', in J. P. Potier and A.
Tiran, *Jean-Baptiste Say: Nouveaux regards sur son oeuvre* (Paris,
2002), pp. 325–59. See also R. Whatmore, *Republicanism and the
French Revolution: An Intellectual History of Jean Baptiste Say's
Political Economy* (Oxford, 2000); R. R. Palmer, *An Economist in
Troubled Times* (Princeton, 1997).

6 On the eighteenth-century discussion of '*doux commerce*' see A.
Hirschmann, *The Passions and the Interests. Political Arguments
for Capitalism before Its Triumph* (Princeton, 1977).

7 B. Constant, 'The Liberty of the Ancients Compared to that
of the Moderns?' [1819], in B. Constant, *Political Writings*, B.
Fontana (ed.) (Cambridge, 1988), pp. 308–29.

8 Say, *Traité d'économie politique*, vol. 2, ch. 7, sect. 5, pp. 92–4.

9 But Say does emphasise the role of machinery in the division of
labour and the importance of advances in the use made of the
powers of nature. It was for this reason also that Say criticised
the term 'commercial society' and preferred to refer to 'industrial
society'. Eventually, he imagined, in 'a perfectly industrial society',
'men without being less numerous, would all be employed
which categorically demanded a certain amount of intelligence,
and where all action which was purely mechanical would be
performed by animals or machines'. See Steiner, 'Le Théorie de la
production', p. 334.

    In the 1814 edition of the *Traité*, there is a brief chapter
arguing the merits of machines both for '*la classe ouvrière*' and,

even more, for consumers. It was stated that many more hands were employed in cotton manufacture in England, France and Germany since their introduction, just as in printing. See vol. 1, ch. 7, pp. 52–61. Say was to elaborate these arguments in the *Cours complet*, as the argument about machinery grew more intense (see below).

10   J. B. Say, *England and the English People*, 2nd edn, J. Richter (trans.) (London, 1816).

11   As above, p. 14.

12   As above, p. 21.

13   As above, pp. 26, 29–30, 30–2.

14   As above, pp. 35, 36, 37–8.

15   As above, p. 38.

16   As above, p. 39.

17   As above, p. 43.

18   As above, pp. 65–6.

19   As above, pp. 63–5.

20   As above, p. 62.

21   See G. Stedman Jones, 'National Bankruptcy and Social Revolution: European Observers on Britain, 1813–1844', in D. Winch & P. O'Brien (eds.), *The Political Economy of British Historical Experience, 1688–1914* (Oxford, 2002), pp. 61–93.

22   M. de Montvéran, *Histoire critique et raisonée de la situation de l'Angleterre au 1e Janvier 1816*, 8 vols. (Paris, 1819), vol. 1, p. 324.

23   M. le Comte Chaptal, *De l'Industrie française*, 2 vols. (Paris, 1819), vol. 2, p. 29.

24   As above, vol. 2, p. 31.

25   As above, vol. 2, pp. 38–40. Chaptal was a chemist as well as a factory owner. He became professor of chemistry at the École Polytechnique. Under the First Empire he acquired a large estate where he pioneered chemical experiments, especially in the cultivation of sugar beet. In 1823 he published *La Chimie appliquée à l'agriculture*. This contrast between France and

England was taken up by N. de Briavoinne in *De l'Industrie en Belgique, causes de décadence et de prosperité* (Brussels, 1839): 'C'est par une sorte d'aveu universel que la France est reconnue le siège de la révolution dans les arts chimiques, l'Angleterre celui de la révolution en mécanique' (p. 192).

26 *Edinburgh Review* 64 (October 1819), p. 367.

27 J. C. L. Simonde de Sismondi, *Nouveaux principes d'économie politique ou de la richesse dans ses rapports avec la population*, 2 vols. (Paris, 1819).

28 As above, vol. 1, p. vi. Sismondi claimed that, pushed beyond a certain point, the division of labour could benefit the entrepreneur, without it producing a comparable advantage to society. 'We have demonstrated that if it is not accompanied by a [comparably] growing demand, the competition which enriches a few individuals produces a certain loss for all the others', as above, vol. 1, pp. 370, 374.

29 J. B. Say, 'Sur la Balance des consommations avec les productions', *Revue Encyclopédique* 23 (1824), pp. 20–1; *Traité d'économie politique*, 2 vols., 1803, vol. 1, p. 80; vol. 2, p. 244; J. C. L. Simonde de Sismondi, 'De la balance des consommations et des productions', *Revue encyclopédique* 22 (1824), p. 281. Cited in P. Steiner, 'Say, les ideologues et le groupe de coppet', *Revue française d'histoire des idées politiques*, no. 18, 2nd. sem. (2003), pp. 331–53.

30 As above, p. 339.

31 As above, p. 341.

32 As above, p. 337.

33 As above, p. 322.

34 As above, p. 323.

35 J. C. L. Simonde de Sismondi, 'Political Economy', Brewster's *Edinburgh Encyclopaedia*, 1815 (New York, 1966), pp. 117–18, 119–20.

36 Sismondi, *Nouveaux principes*, vol. 2, p. 262.

37   As above, vol. 1, p. 146.

38   As above, vol. 2, p. 262.

39   As above, vol. 2, p. 305. In a later work, *Études sur les sciences sociales* (1836, 1838), Sismondi provided the following definition of 'pauperism' – the word which dominated French and German discussion of the condition of the 'proletarian' in the 1820s–50s: '*Pauperism* is a calamity which began by making itself felt in England, and which has at present no other name but what the English have given it, though it begins to visit also other industrial countries. Pauperism is the state to which proletaries [*sic*] are necessarily reduced when work fails. It is the condition of men who must live by their labour, who can only work when capitalists employ them and who, when they are idle, must become a burden on the community' (*Political Economy and the Philosophy of Government; a Series of Essays Selected from the Works of M. de Sismondi*) (London, 1847), p. 149).

40   As above, vol. 2, p. 350.

41   As above, vol. 1, p. 368. Here is the probable origin of the notion, found in the *Communist Manifesto*, that proletarians have no country.

42   *Agriculture toscane*, cited in Sismondi, *Political Economy and the Philosophy of Government*, p. 31.

43   J. C. L. Simonde de Sismondi, *Histoire des républiques italiennes du moyen âge*, 16 vols. (Paris, 1807–24).

44   See above, p. 32.

45   From the introduction to *Études* in Sismondi, *Political Economy and the Philosophy of Government*, p. 139.

46   Sismondi, *Nouveaux principes*, vol. 2, p. 401.

47   This complaint about the disappearance of intermediate social strata and the increasingly stark polarisation of rich and poor was endlessly repeated in the literature of social criticism between 1820 and 1848. See, for instance, the treatment of this

theme in the *Communist Manifesto*, G. Stedman Jones (ed.),
Karl Marx & Friedrich Engels, *The Communist Manifesto*
(London, 2002), p. 231.

48 Sismondi, *Nouveaux principes*, vol. 2, p. 359.

49 As above, vol. 1, p. 362.

50 As above, p. 45.

51 As above, vol. 2, p. 366.

52 Sismondi, *Political Economy and the Philosophy of Government*.
The only other complete text by Sismondi available in
English, his article of 1815 on political economy for Brewster's
Edinburgh Encyclopaedia, provided no more than hints of the
critical position he would adopt in *Nouveaux principes*.

53 In France, see for example the *Éloge* of Sismondi by Mignet,
translated in *Political Economy and the Philosophy of
Government*, pp. 1–25, and Michelet's tribute: 'His glory is to
have pointed out the evils; courage was necessary for that! – to
have foretold new crises. But the remedy? That is not an affair
of the same man, or the same age. Five hundred years have
been required to set us free from political feudalism; will a few
years be sufficient to set us free from industrial feudalism?'
(as above, p. 42). For German discussion of the notion of the
'proletariat' in the 1830s and 1840s see W. Conze, 'Von "Pöbel"
zum "Proletariat"', in H. U. Wehler (ed.), *Moderne deutsche
Sozialgeschichte* (Cologne, 1973), pp. 111–37. For Sismondi's
impact upon legitimist social criticism, see A. de Villeneuve-
Bargemont, *Économie politique chrétienne*, 3 vols. (Paris, 1834).

54 J. B. Say, *Letters to T. R. Malthus on Political Economy and
Stagnation of Commerce*, H. Laski (ed.) (London, 1936), p. 8;
see also D. Winch, *Riches and Poverty: An Intellectual History
of Political Economy in Britain 1750–1834* (Cambridge, 1996), pt
III.

55 Say, *Letters to T. R. Malthus*, p. 9.

56 As above.

57   J. C. L. Simonde de Sismondi, *Nouveaux principes d'économie politique ou de la richesse dans ses rapports avec la population* (Paris, 1827). In a new preface Sismondi considered his position vindicated by the course of the 1825–6 depression, which included riots against the power loom in Lancashire: '[S]even years have passed by and the facts seem to me to have vindicated me. They have proved much more than I could have done, that the savants, from whom I separated myself, were in pursuit of a false prosperity' (p. ii). According to Sismondi's journal, in the later 1820s Say was coming round to the Sismondi position: '5th September 1828 – I have had a letter from M. Say, who announces to me a second volume of his book with some concessions to my principles on the limit of production', *Political Economy and the Philosophy of Government*, p. 449.

58   J. B. Say, *Cours complet d'économie politique pratique*, 6 vols. (Paris, 1828), vol. 1, p. 364.

59   As above, pp. 390–1.

60   As above, pp. 393–4.

61   As above, p. 395.

62   As above, pp. 396–7.

63   As above, p. 398.

64   As above, p. 399.

65   As above, p. 400.

66   As above, p. 401.

67   As above.

68   As above, p. 412.

69   As above, p. 416.

70   As above, pp. 418–19.

71   As above, pp. 420–1.

72   See D. C. Coleman, *Myth, History and the Industrial Revolution* (London, 1992), pp. 1–43.

Chapter V

1 J. Blanqui, *Histoire de l'économie politique* (Brussels, 1842), ch. 38.

2 See L. Say (ed.), *Nouveaux dictionnaire d'économie politique*, (Paris, 1891), p. 197; *Dictionnaire de biographie française* (Paris, 1954), p. 643.

3 Blanqui, *Histoire de l'économie politique*, p. 167.

4 As above, p. 173.

5 As above, p. 173.

6 As above, p. 173.

7 As above, p. 180.

8 As above, p. 180. The new 'social school' of French economists was defined by the fact it 'related all progress to the general perfection of society' (see above, p. 297). Blanqui included in his 'social school' not only those mainly inspired by Sismondi, like Villeneuve-Bargemont and Droz, but also those such as Charles Dunoyer and Charles Comte who followed Say (see above, ch. 41).

9 As above, p. 181.

10 As above, p. 183.

11 As above, p. 205.

12 As above, p. 169.

13 As above, p. 203.

14 M. Villermé, *Tableau de l'état physique et moral des ouvriers employés dans les manufactures de coton, de laine et de soie*, 2 vols. (Paris, 1840), vol. 2, pp. 169–92, 281–2.

15 E. Buret, *De la misère des classes laborieuses en Angleterre et en France* (Brussels, 1842), p. 596.

16 Blanqui, *Histoire de l'économie politique*, pp. 204–5.

17 L. von Stein, *Der Sozialismus und Communismus des heutigen Frankreichs*, 2 vols., 2nd edn (Leipzig, 1848), vol. 1, p. 166.

18 Blanqui, *Histoire de l'économie politique*, p. 167.

19   'Introductory Discourse', in J. R. McCulloch (ed.), Adam Smith,
      An Enquiry into the Nature and Causes of the Wealth of Nations
      (London, 1850), pp. liii–liv.

20   *Edinburgh Review* 46 (June–October 1827), p. 1.

21   As above, pp. 1–2.

22   H. Martineau, *The History of England during the Thirty Years'
      Peace, 1816–1846*, 2 vols., London (1849–50), vol. 2, p. 708.

23   G. R. Porter, *The Progress of the Nation in Its Various Social and
      Economic Relations from the Beginning of the Nineteenth Century*
      (London, 1847), p. 178.

24   See N. F. R. Crafts, 'British Economic Growth, 1700–1831: A
      Review of the Evidence', *Economic History Review* 36 (1983),
      pp. 177–99; Crafts, 'The New Economic History and the
      Industrial Revolution', in P. Mathias & J. A. Davis (eds.), *The
      First Industrial Revolutions* (Oxford, 1989); C. K. Harley, 'British
      Industrialisation before 1841: Evidence of Slow Growth during
      the Industrial Revolution', *Journal of Economic History*, 42
      (1982); Harley, 'Re-assessing the Industrial Revolution: A Macro
      View', in J. Mokyr (ed.), *The British Industrial Revolution: An
      Economic Perspective* (Boulder, Co., 1993); N. F. R. Crafts & C. K.
      Harley, 'Output Growth and the British Industrial Revolution:
      A Restatement of the Crafts–Harley View', *Economic History
      Review* 45 (1993).

25   See E. Baines, *History of the Cotton Manufacture of Great Britain*
      (London, 1835); P. Gaskell, *The Manufacturing Population of
      England* (London, 1833); A. Ure, *The Philosophy of Manufactures*
      (London, 1835); Porter, *The Progress of the Nation*.

26   Nassau W. Senior, *An Outline of the Science of Political Economy*
      (London, 1836), p. 72.

27   For an account, see M. Berg, *The Machinery Question and the
      Making of Political Economy 1815–1848* (London, 1980), pt II.

28   As above, pp. 111–44.

29   Ure, *The Philosophy of Manufactures*, pp. 14–15.

30 As above, p. 19; and see K. Marx, *Capital*, Karl Marx & Friedrich Engels, *Collected Works*, vol. 35 (London, 1996), ch. 15, p. 435.

31 E. A. Wrigley, *Continuity, Chance and Change: The Character of the Industrial Revolution in England* (Cambridge, 1988); N. von Tunzelmann, *Steam Power and British Industrialisation to 1860* (Oxford, 1978).

32 Berg, *The Machinery Question*, p. 132.

33 B. Hilton, *The Age of Atonement: The Influence of Evangelicalism on Social and Economic Thought 1785–1865* (Oxford, 1988), p. 69.

34 W. Huskisson, *The Speeches of the Right Honourable William Huskisson with a Biographical Memoir*, 3 vols. (London, 1831), vol. 3, pp. 670–1.

35 As above, pp. 671–2.

36 Porter, *The Progress of the Nation*, pp. 478–9.

37 Blanqui, *Histoire de l'économie politique*, pp. 252–3.

38 As above, p. 250; see also Marx's reference to 'the cynical Ricardo' in K. Marx, 'Critical Marginal Notes on the Article, the King of Prussia and Social Reform, by a "Prussian"', Karl Marx & Friedrich Engels, *Collected Works*, vol. 3, p. 192.

39 Blanqui, *Histoire de l'économie politique*, pp. 252–3

40 J. R. McCulloch, *A Treatise on the Principles and Practical Influence of Taxation and the Funding System* (London, 1845), p. 110. On McCulloch's attitude to child labour, see D. P. O'Brien, *J. R. McCulloch: A Study in Classical Economics* (London, 1970), p. 371.

41 Martineau, *The History of England*, vol. 2, p. 715.

42 R. Owen, 'An Address to the Working Classes, April 15 1819', in R. Owen, *A New View of Society and Other Writings*, G. D. H. Cole (ed.) (London, 1927), p. 150.

43 R. Owen, 'Observations on the Effect of the Manufacturing System', in G. Claeys (ed.), Robert Owen, *A New View of Society and Other Writings* (Harmondsworth, 1991), p. 94.

44 W. Hazlitt, *Political Essays* (London, 1819), p. 103.

45   *Edinburgh Review* 64 (October 1819), pp. 453–77.

46   As above, pp. 474–5.

47   As above, p. 468.

48   As above, p. 468.

49   As above, p. 468.

50   Sismondi, *Nouveaux principes*, 2nd edn, vol. 2, p. 365.

51   *Edinburgh Review* 35 (March–July 1821), p. 110.

52   M. Agulhon, *1848, ou l'apprentissage de la république 1848–1852* (Paris, 1975), p. 10.

53   J. Stillinger (ed.), John Stuart Mill, *Autobiography* (Oxford, 1971), pp. 39, 64–5, 69, 117–18.

54   Richard Cobden to Joseph Sturge, 25 July 1842, cited in W. Hinde, *Richard Cobden: A Victorian Outsider* (Yale, 1987), p. 114.

55   Mill, *Autobiography*, p. 64.

56   J. S. Mill, *Principles of Political Economy with Some of Their Applications to Social Philosophy*, 2 vols., 3rd edn (London, 1857), vol. 1, pp. 447–8.

57   T. Carlyle, *Past and Present* (London, 1843), ch. 1, 'Midas', pp. 1–8.

58   Blanqui, *Histoire de l'économie politique*, p. 153.

59   R. Carlile, *The Life of Thomas Paine Written Purposely to Bind with His Writings*, 2nd edn (London, 1821), p. 23.

60   G. Stedman Jones, 'The Labours of Henry Mayhew, Metropolitan Correspondent', *London Journal* vol. 10, no. 1 (1984), p. 82; H. Mayhew, *London Labour and the London Poor*, 4 vols., 1861 edn, vol. 2, p. 325; vol. 3, p. 309.

61   J. M. Baernreither, *English Associations of Working Men* (London, 1889), p. 167. See also J. Thompson, 'A nearly related people: German views of the British Labour Market, 1870–1900, in D. Winch and P. K. O'Brien, *The Political Economy of British Historical Experience, 1688–1914* (Oxford 2002).

62   For an excellent account of the difficulties of friendly societies, see P. Gosden, *The Friendly Societies in England 1815–1875* (Manchester, 1961), ch. 4 & *passim*. See also Barry Supple

(1974), 'Legislation and Virtue: An Essay on Working Class
Self-Help and the State in the Early Nineteenth Century'. In
Neil McKendrick, ed., *Historical Perspectives: Studies in English
Thought and Society* (London: Europa, 1974), pp. 211–254.

63 Gosden, *Friendly Societies*, p. 97.

Chapter VI

1 Cited in A. Gueslin, *L'Invention de l'économie sociale: le XIXe
siècle français* (Paris, 1987), p. 94.

2 See F. Burdeau, *Histoire de l'administration française: du 18e au
20e siècle*, 2nd edn (Paris, 1994), pp. 145–9.

3 See Gueslin, *L'Invention de l'économie sociale*, pp. 161–6; see
also P. Schöttler, *Naissance des Bourses du Travail* (Paris, 1985);
C. Topalov, *Naissance du Chômeur 1880–1910* (Paris, 1994).

4 J. M. Mayeur and Madeleine Rebérioux, *The Third Republic
from Its Origins to the Great War 1871–1914* (Cambridge, 1975),
p. 323.

5 Cited in R. D. Anderson, *France 1870–1914: Politics and Society*
(London, 1977), p. 96.

6 S. Webb, *Socialism in England* (London, 1890); *The History of
Trade Unionism* (London, 1894), p. 361; and see also J. Saville,
'Henry George and the British Labour Movement', *Bulletin of
the Society for the Study of Labour History* 5 (Autumn 1962),
pp. 18–26.

7 H. George, *Progress and Poverty: An Inquiry into the Cause
of Industrial Depressions and of Increase of Want with the
Increase of Wealth … The Remedy* (1879) (New York, 1987),
p. 560; the impact of Henry George on late nineteenth-century
radicalism was worldwide from Tolstoy to John Dewey. It is
generally forgotten how important a part his ideas played on
the prehistory of the Labour Party and of New Liberalism
in Britain. See, for example, the testimony of Keir Hardie,
who wrote in 1906 that his reading of *Progress and Poverty*

and George's visit to Scotland in 1884–5 'unlocked many of
the industrial and economic difficulties which then beset the
worker trying to take an intelligent interest in his own affairs'
('Character Sketches. 1. The Labour Party and the Books
that Have Helped to Make It', *The Review of Reviews* (June
1906), p. 571). Or Bernard Shaw, who later wrote to George's
daughter, 'Your father found me a literary dilettante and
militant rationalist in religion, and a barren rascal at that. By
turning my mind to economics he made a man of me' (cited in
Agnes George de Mille, 'Preface', *Progress and Poverty*, p. xiii).

8   George, *Progress and Poverty*, pp. 508, 557; on its impact upon
discussion of the housing crisis in London in the 1880s, see G.
Stedman Jones, *Outcast London: A Study in the Relationship
between Classes in Victorian Society* (Oxford, 1971), ch. 11.

9   Hypatia Bradlaugh Bonner, *Charles Bradlaugh: A Record of
His Life and Work by His Daughter* (1894), 7th edn (London,
1908), pp. 170, 172; H. M. Hyndman & Charles Bradlaugh, *Will
Socialism Benefit the English People?* (London, 1884), p. 17.

10 See G. Searle, *The Quest for National Efficiency* (Oxford, 1971);
Stedman Jones, *Outcast London*, pt III.

11 W. E. Blackley, 'National Insurance: A Cheap, Practical, and
Popular Means of Abolishing Poor Rates', *The Nineteenth
Century* 4 (July–Nov. 1878), pp. 835–9.

12 On the origins of the welfare legislation of the Liberal
governments of 1906–14, see B. R. Gilbert, *The Evolution
of National Insurance in Great Britain: The Origins of the
Welfare State* (London, 1966); P. Thane, 'Contributory
vs. Non-contributory Old Age Pensions, 1878–1908, in
P. Thane (ed.), *The Origins of British Social Policy* (London,
1978); 'The Working Class and State "Welfare" in Britain,
1880–1914', *Historical Journal* 27 (1984) pp. 877–900; P. Thane,
'Government and Society in England and Wales, 1750–1914', in
F. M. L. Thompson (ed.), *Cambridge Social History of Britain*

1750–1950, vol. 3, *Social Agencies and Institutions* (Cambridge, 1990), pp. 1–63; J. Harris, 'From Poor Law to Welfare State? A European Perspective', in D. Winch & P. O'Brien (eds.), *The Political Economy of British Historical Experience, 1688–1914* (Oxford, 2002), pp. 409–39.

13   See W. J. Mommsen (ed.), *The Emergence of the Welfare State in Britain and Germany 1850–1950* (London, 1981); E. P. Hennock, *British Social Reform and German Precedents: The Case of Social Insurance 1880–1914* (Oxford, 1987).

14   On the Poor Law reforms of the late 1860s and early 1870s, see M. E. Rose, 'The Crisis of Poor Relief in England 1860–1890', in Mommsen, *The Emergence of the Welfare State*, pp. 50–71.

15   Revd & Mrs Samuel A. Barnett, *Practicable Socialism: Essays on Social Reform* (London, 1888), pp. 191–9. On the intellectual and political character of turn-of-the-century social democracy, see P. Clarke, *Liberals and Social Democrats* (Cambridge, 1978); S. Collini, *Liberalism and Sociology* (Cambridge, 1979); E. Bragini and A. Reid, *Currents of radicalism, poplar radicalism, organised labour and party politics 1850–1914* (Cambridge, 1991).

16   A. Toynbee, *Lectures on the Industrial Revolution in England: Popular Addresses, Notes and Other Fragments* (London, 1884), pp. 11, 14, 17, 83, 84, 85, 88, 93. On Toynbee, see Alon Kadish, *Apostle Arnold: The Life and Death of Arnold Toynbee, 1852–83* (Durham, NC, 1986). On the development of negative evaluations of industrialisation, see M. J. Wiener, *English Culture and the Decline of the Industrial Spirit 1850–1980* (Cambridge, 1981).

17   Toynbee, *Industrial Revolution*, pp. xv–xvi, 20, 21, 25, 86, 87, 109, 114, 146.

INDEX